simply®

Feng Shui

simply®

Feng Shui

SARA BARTLETT

STERLING/ZAMBEZI
An imprint of Sterling Publishing Co., Inc.

New York / London
www.sterlingpublishing.com

STERLING and the distinctive Sterling logo are registered trademarks of
Sterling Publishing Co., Inc.

Library of Congress Cataloging-in-Publication Data

Bartlett, Sarah.
Simply Feng shui / Sarah Bartlett.
p. cm.
ISBN 978-1-4027-5457-9
1. Feng shui. I. Title.
BF1779.F4B38 2009
133.3'337--dc22
2009015607

2   4   6   8   10   9   7   5   3   1

Published by Sterling Publishing Co., Inc.
387 Park Avenue South, New York, NY 10016
Text © 2010 by Sarah Bartlett
Illustrations © 2010 Adam Reiti
Distributed in Canada by Sterling Publishing
c/o Canadian Manda Group, 165 Dufferin Street
Toronto, Ontario, Canada M6K 3H6
Published in the UK solely by Zambezi Publishing Ltd.
P.O. Box 221, Plymouth, PL2 2EQ
Distributed in Australia by Capricorn Link (Australia) Pty. Ltd.
P.O. Box 704, Windsor, NSW 2756, Australia

Sterling ISBN 978-1-4027-5457-9
Zambezi ISBN 978-1-903065-66-2

For information about custom editions, special sales, premium and corporate
purchases, please contact Sterling Special Sales Department at 800-805-5489 or
specialsales@sterlingpublishing.com.

contents

introduction

This book is a simple guide to the Chinese art of Feng Shui. It provides you with lots of tips and secrets that you can use right away to improve your lifestyle. By harmonizing and changing the spaces in your home, not only will you enhance your personal energy for emotional, physical, and material well-being, but you will also bring good fortune into your life.

WHAT IS FENG SHUI?

Feng Shui (pronounced *foong shway*) is the ancient Chinese art of furniture and object placement to create positive energy flow around the home. A harmonious home means a harmonious lifestyle. The ancient Chinese believed that the world, humankind, and all of nature were connected by a flow of universal energy called *Ch'i*. (The Indian equivalent is *prana*; the Japanese, *ki*). This Ch'i was made up of two qualities, "feng" and "shui." "Feng" means wind and "shui" means water. Feng, or wind, energy is active, dynamic, yang energy; shui, or water, energy is passive, receptive, yin energy. It was the channeling and harmonizing of these two forces in nature that became known as Feng Shui to the ancient mystics. More than three thousand years ago, the Taoist mystics used Feng Shui to determine auspicious locations for ancestral tombs, as well as to enhance their sexual energy. According to the Taoists, the key to long life and happiness was to be found through energizing the flow of Ch'i during lovemaking.

Many Eastern cultures have over the centuries relied on the art and science of Feng Shui to plan sites for houses, offices, gardens, and interiors. This practice has now become popular in the West, and we can use these basic principles and tried-and-true methods to achieve harmonious energy in the home. This process enhances our well-being and creates beneficial energy to improve our lives.

HOW DOES IT WORK?

Ch'i flows everywhere. It is a universal unseen force that flows through the environment and our bodies. Many Eastern therapies, such as shiatsu, acupuncture, and Chinese herbal medicine, are based on this energy system. Practitioners subtly change the energy flow within the body to remove blockages or stagnant areas that could create illness. Similarly, Ch'i can flow through a garden, down the road, and into your home, but for you to benefit from the energy in your living space, the currents need to be free to flow throughout the home; blocked or stagnant energy spots create disharmony.

Ch'i energy always moves in spirals, and this movement needs to be enhanced. Negative energy, called "Sha Ch'i" moves in straight lines and is referred to as "secret arrows" in Feng Shui. This is why sharp corners, beams, and straight lines in the home need to be modified, changed, or given a "cure" to create a flowing environment.

There are several different schools of Feng Shui thought. One is based on a scientific and classical approach that uses astronomy, astrology, and a powerful Chinese compass called a "Lo Pan". Another concentrates solely on cures and enhancements, and a third is a blend of intuition and spiritual awareness. This book shows you how to try out some of the simpler principles of this highly organized system. Remember that the changes you make or create in your home are intended to make the energy work for your benefit.

Lo Pan.

1

MAKING A START

Before you do anything, you must first clear away any negative or bad energy that's been dormant in the house, home, or workplace. If you want to start afresh, there's nothing like clearing out all the clutter and cleansing the spaces of your home and hearth.

DECLUTTERING

To accomplish this task successfully, you have to be ruthless with yourself and your family, so approach each room in turn and decide whether you really need those things that are piling up in the closets. You might even have boxes full of things you've forgotten about stored in the attic or cellar, so don't neglect these areas, as they can harbor stagnant or negative energy. Before steaming in with the vacuum cleaner and the trash bags, though, understand why you are doing this, because understanding the process is as essential as doing it. Also bear in mind that while it may feel difficult to throw things out, once the junk is gone, it's remarkable how quickly you'll forget about it. The number of possessions you have is also a symbol of the type of person you are. The more junk you hoard, the more likely it is you need to reassess your values. Why are you so acquisitive? Do you feel insecure without possessions? Similarly, if you live in a minimalist cell, you might need to ask whether your values incorporate the needs of others.

Once you have decluttered your home, you'll feel not only virtuous but also excited about the fresh start you're making on this new phase in your life. Now you need to cleanse the empty spaces of your home and revitalize the home with positive energy.

SPACE-CLEARING TECHNIQUES

There are many ways to clear away negative energy and re-vitalize the home. Here are some suggestions. If you don't like one idea, then try another that suits you better. Some individuals might like clapping, while others might like purging with candles or incense, so take your pick.

1. Burning

Cleanse a whole house or room by burning small perfumed candles in each room. Let the candle burn right down before you extinguish it. Alternatively, use incense—sandalwood, lavender, and geranium essences are the best fragrances, but this is a matter of personal taste. Candles burn away negative energy and reconnect vibrations and an atmo-sphere that is reflective of you. Use colors that are suited to your needs, for example, white for purification and clarifica-tion, red for passion, blue for career prospects, green for friendship, yellow for good communication.

Note: Be very careful not to leave any burning candles unattended when you leave a room, as this could present a significant fire danger.

2. Clapping

Walk around the room or house and clap your hands briskly and rhythmically. Don't forget to clap in dark corners and at ceiling height, too. The sound of your hands will become a mantra for the energy, and you will soon start to feel the energy shifting and becoming clearer.

3. Sweeping

In Malaysia, Feng Shui practitioners often used an old bird-of-paradise nest that they tied to the end of a piece of twine and then whirled around in the air. However, a broom or a large spray of dead branches will work equally well. Lift the

broom and sweep it through the air to stir and disperse any negative energy. Another method is to move your hands with open fingers through the air; if you feel any resistance, just push it away with wide sweeping movements of your arms.

4. Laid-Back Space Clearing

Sit cross-legged on the floor. Write a letter to the room or home and tell it that the changes you are about to make are functional, beneficial, and spiritual. Convey that the energy needs to be channeled for the benefit of you, your home, your workplace, and the world. Once you've read your letter out loud to the room, burn it or bury it in grand ceremonial style.

5. Touching

Touch all the things you are going to keep. Give them a name and make them feel wanted and loved. Touch the walls and the floor, too. This emotional contact with inanimate objects may sound silly, but you are acknowledging the presence of everything in the home, which has its own hidden positive energy, too. This way any negative energy will be dispelled.

6. Bell Ringing

Hold a thought of goodness and clarity in your mind. Begin ringing a bell as you circle the room. The sound waves will carry your thoughts to every part of the room. Finally, close the energies of the room down by moving the bell in a huge circle or a figure-eight shape in the middle of the room. For those of you who practice spiritual, psychic, or heading work, this is like closing your psychic center at the end of a session.

ABOUT YIN AND YANG

Yin and yang are complementary energies in Chinese philosophy. They are the source of the Ch'i as it flows through the universe. The Taoist Tai Ch'i symbol, a circle, creates a unity between the black and white areas. Yin is dark and passive, usually associated with the feminine and receptivity, and yang is white, positive, extrovert energy and usually associated with the masculine. Within each section, there is also the circle of its complementary energy, so in yin we find yang and in yang we find yin. The symbol reveals that nothing is ever totally yin or totally yang, but a combination of them both.

Yin's qualities traditionally have been associated with water, the moon, stillness, cold, and darkness, whereas yang relates to the sun, fire, bright light, and movement.

In the earliest Feng Shui schools, the environment was more important than the home iself. Yin represented the north side of a mountain, lakes, or shady places where not much sun was found, while yang landscapes were south-facing slopes and sunny places. Mountains are usually yin and water is usually yang, because water moves (unless it's a still lake or pond; then it's considered yin).

In modern Feng Shui, assessing yin and yang energies is useful for getting the general feel of the home. Is your home more yin or more yang? Does it have lots of light or not enough? Traditionally a home is considered to be more yin than yang. This is because it is usually a place of calm, peace, and retreat from the world. Nowadays many people work from home, so it's important to activate a more dynamic yang feel to the office or work area with yang colors such as reds and orange and bright lights to balance the yin feel of the home.

If you live in the countryside, there will be more receptive yin energy around you, but if you live in a city center surrounded by skyscrapers, in a town, or in the suburbs, then the environment will be highly charged with yang energy. If you live in a city, you need to encourage more yin into your home by introducing soft furnishings, fabric wall hangings, huge, comfy cushions, and soft, earthy colors. You can also enhance yin with soft music and lighting, but don't negate all the yang energy. You need some in the main living space for positive well-being, so yang items such as glass dishes, metal ornaments, stone sculptures, and mirrors can be included in the living or dining room. Keep yang items, including electrical goods, televisions, stereos, and work-related machines, out of the bedroom. Encourage positive yang energy in the kitchen and the hallway by hanging wind chimes, using bright lighting or electrical gadgets, or hanging metal objects on the kitchen wall.

Harmonizing the two qualities of yin and yang throughout the home will encourage the Ch'i to flow more easily and can create happiness and good relationships in your life. These are the basics of good Feng Shui and they'll get you off to a balanced start.

2

THE BAGUA

Apart from yin and yang, there are two very important keys to Feng Shui. One is called the "Bagua" and the other relates to the five elements of Chinese astrology. The relationship that connects the five elements, the Bagua and the direction of your home is the key to harmony. First let's look at the Bagua.

The Bagua is an instant map for finding out where to change things for the better in your home. This ancient grid system (usually pronounced *baagwa*; also spelled *"Pa-Kua)* represents the invisible patterns of energy that are contained within anything from a city block to a landscape, a house, a room, or even a bed. By using this grid, we can see which areas need attention.

The Bagua is based on an ancient Chinese magic number square. According to tradition, about four thousand years

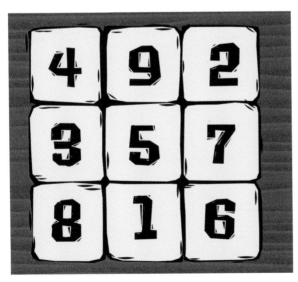

ago, a tortoise emerged from a river. On its back were special markings, which were interpreted as being the numbers 1 to 9. When these numbers are placed in the magic square in the proper formation, every row, whether horizontal, vertical, or diagonal, adds up to 15, and this mathematical "accident" supposedly renders the magic square and its uses magical.

Magic square.

One reason this is an auspicious number is that 15 is the number of days between the new moon and the full moon, which also marks the twenty-four phases of the Chinese year. This highly regarded time cycle was used in ancient traditional divination methods to determine auspicious times to sow seeds, work on gardens, or build houses.

When these same numbers are used to create the octagonal shape of the Bagua, each of the numbers correlates to a keyword.

Octagonal Bagua.

my Feng Shui

THE NINE BAGUA ENERGIES

The keywords listed here correspond to the nine energies or pathways according to their compass points on
the Bagua:

South:	Fire	Fame, success, acknowledgment
Southwest:	Earth	Marriage, love, romantic happiness
West:	Metal	Children, creativity
Northwest:	Metal	Communication, friends, mentors
North:	Water	Career, profession
Northeast:	Earth	Education, knowledge
East:	Wood	Family, well-being
Southeast:	Wood	Wealth, prosperity
Core:	Life energy	

Most schools of Feng Shui use only the eight compass-point
energies, but several use the center of the Bagua, which I've
called the *core*. This area is very important in the home because it represents the heart of the home and the essence
of you. When we enhance this area of the home, we're energizing our innermost selves.

We all have vitality and energy, and the Ch'i flows through us
as it does around our homes. That's why we need to remember that when we're working on areas in our home, we're
balancing and empowering ourselves simultaneously.

HOW TO USE THE BAGUA

The next thing to do is to line up the Bagua over a plan of your home or just the room you're trying to improve. By following these easy steps, you can find out where the nine Bagua energies are located in your home. Start by deciding which areas of your life you feel need improvement or development. Next, you can apply simple Feng Shui enhancers to promote happiness, harmony, and well-being.

1. Draw a rough plan of your home or room.

2. Find the central point of the room or house. If it's irregular, square off the missing areas to make an imaginary regular shape.

3. Draw two diagonal lines from the corners. Where they cross is the center of the space and corresponds to the core area of the Bagua.

4. Find out which direction your home faces so that you can align your plan with the Bagua's north, south, east, and west.

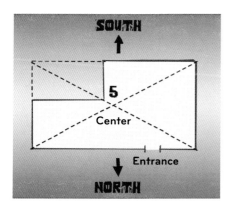

The Bagua over a house with an irregular shape.

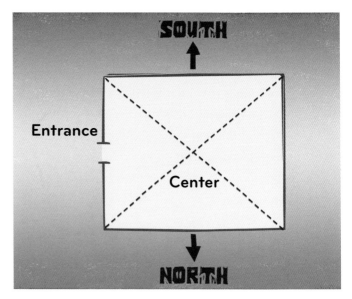

The Bagua over a house with a regular shape.

The easiest way to link the Bagua to your home is to use a compass. Once you have found north, mark it on your drawing, and then add east, west, and south in the appropriate spots. Next, you can write in northeast, northwest, southeast, and southwest.

Even if you don't have a compass, you can figure out which direction your home faces by watching the sun and noting where it rises (east) and where it sets (west). Mark these locations on your home plan, and then you can align your Bagua to these compass points.

Next, copy or trace a Bagua illustration onto tracing paper, or photocopy it onto the kind of transparency you would use on an overhead projector, and then place it over the plan of your home. Make sure you match up the compass points on your plan with the Bagua directions. For example, if your front door is facing south, line up the south/fire/fame part of the Bagua with the front door on your house plan. Then, obviously, the north/water/career area of the Bagua corresponds to the home's kitchen.

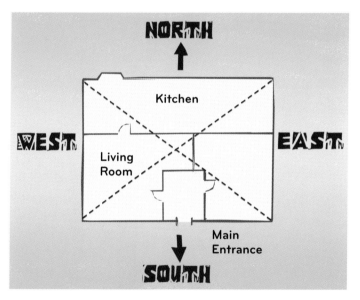

The Bagua over the plan of a home.

MISSING SPACES AND PROJECTIONS

Some rooms and many homes don't form simple rectangles or squares, so you may have to contract or expand the Bagua to fit unusually shaped homes or rooms, or houses with extensions. For example, a house may have a missing space due to two extensions; this means that the west area of the Bagua, which relates to creativity and children, falls outside the home.

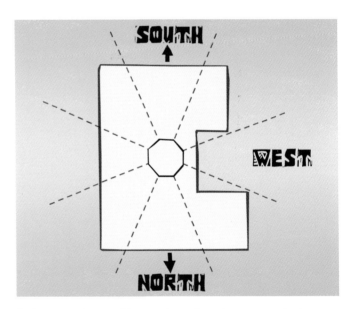

A house where the extension has created a missing space. Here the Bagua area west/ children falls outside the house.

MAPPING OUT ROOMS

You can use the Bagua to map out an individual room in order to enhance specific energies relevant to that room. For example, you might want to create a more passionate or loving intimacy in the bedroom, so placing specific enhancers in the southwest corner of the room (which corresponds to marriage, love, and romantic happiness) would be beneficial.

In the kitchen, you might want to create an atmosphere that encourages great home cooking and good family conversations, so placing specific enhancers in the east (family and well-being) and northeast (education and knowledge) corners would be beneficial.

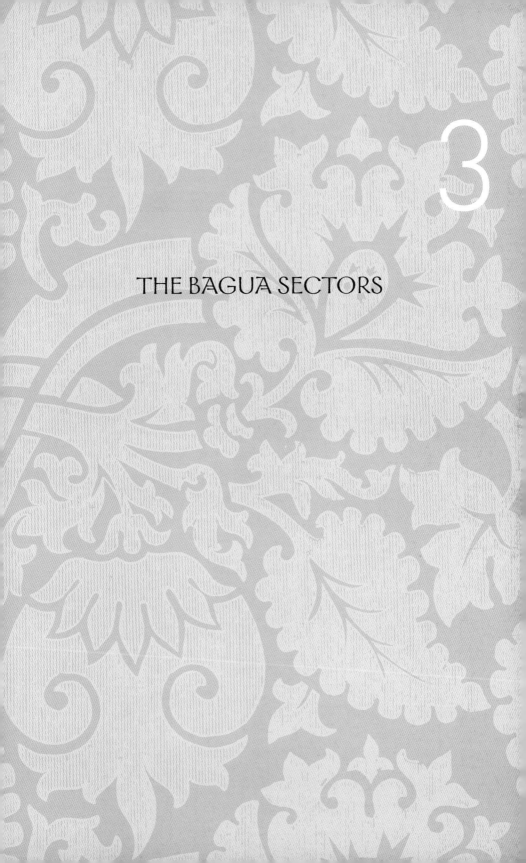

3

THE BAGUA SECTORS

The nine sectors of the Bagua relate to nine areas of your house, and these in turn link with nine aspects of your life. If an aspect of your life is making you unhappy, you'll find out how to link that aspect to a relevant sector your house. You will then find out how to make a start on changing things for the better.

ANSWER THE FOLLOWING QUESTIONS

1. Do you want to get ahead in your career or change it completely? If the answer is yes, you must reinforce the NORTH area.

2. Do you want your talents to be noticed, or do you want to have great success from one of your skills? If the answer is yes, reinforce the SOUTH sector.

3. Do you feel you have too many money problems or you just want to be more prosperous? If the answer is yes, reinforce the SOUTHEAST area.

4. Do you want family relationships to work better, or do you just want a general improved sense of well-being for yourself and all who live on the premises? If the answer is yes, reinforce the EAST area.

5. Are you keen to have children? Do you have creative urges or want to create something new in your life? If so, reinforce the WEST area.

6. Do you want to meet the perfect partner or find new romance? Do you want to improve your

intimate love relationship or find a better balance and harmony between you and your lover? If so, reinforce the SOUTHWEST corner of your home.

7. Do you want to improve your mind? Do you seek wisdom or want to explore other philosophies spiritually or intellectually? Do you want to pass an exam or achieve something in education? If so, reinforce the NORTHEAST corner of your home.

8. Do you want to improve communication channels, make new contacts, or boost your interactive skills? If so, reinforce the NORTHWEST corner of your home.

9. Do you want to know yourself better, begin to live out your true potential, and feel at one with yourself? If so, enhance the CORE of your home.

Find the area that you want to improve, but don't try to do too much at once; Feng Shui is about balancing energies, not overdoing one at the expense of others.

NORTH: CAREER

Key element: The north sector of your home is reinforced by a water enhancement.

To make your professional life work more smoothly or to promote beneficial energy in your career, use a simple water feature such as images of fish, an aquarium, or a blue bowl.

Harmony in the North Sector

The north sector of your home probably has much less light than the south, so it's important to avoid drabness. Don't use the colors that are associated with the water element, which are dark blue and black. Also, it's important not to overemphasize water, or you'll find yourself working day and night and never getting any peace. If you have too great a water enhancement, you'll end up believing that your career takes precedence over every other aspect of your life, a belief that can be detrimental to relationships.

Metal and wood elements are both compatible with water, so you can introduce a little of both to balance the general atmosphere of this part of your home. A small feature of trickling water over stones and some small upright plants is one possible choice. Alternatively, brighten up the north sector of your home with metal items, such as stainless-steel objects, gold- or silver-framed pictures, or a bowl of coins, all of which are highly auspicious for financial success in your career.

The bedroom is a special case, as you want to avoid anything to do with commerce and careers in this area. Avoid medium or dark blue colors if your bedroom is in the north of the home. The bedroom should be a place of rest and calm, and blue can evoke bad dreams and erratic sleep patterns.

SOUTH: FAME AND FORTUNE

Key element: Using fire enhancements will reinforce the south area of your home.

The south represents brightness and happiness, and it has a summery, yang energy. It's the sector of your home that, if harmonized, will bring everyone in the household external recognition and a sense of achievement. To boost your reputation and to enhance your talents and chances for success, use a fire feature in this part of your home, such as the color red, a photo of a red sunrise, or any redbird imagery. Redbirds are highly auspicious in Feng Shui.

Harmony in the South Sector

You probably get most natural light in the south of your home. The corresponding color for the south direction is red, so you don't want to add more red here, or you may bring anger and unsettled emotions into the home. To balance the spirited fiery energy of this part of your home, use wood and earth objects here. Too much fame can make you self-centered and intolerant, so it's important to incorporate earth and wood balancers such as soft ochres and dusky desert yellows, along with antiques, plants, and books. This combination will give you a far more realistic sense of what fame and fortune mean to you, while still encouraging high self-esteem and achievement of personal goals without overinflating your sense of importance.

SOUTHEAST: WEALTH AND PROSPERITY

Key element: The southeast area of your home is reinforced using wood enhancements.

Place images in greens and yellows here to promote a sense of wealth and to improve your financial situation. To really give this area a boost, place a money plant, also called a jade plant, near a window.

Harmony in the Southeast Sector

The Chinese consider the southeast area of the home the most important because it represents the family's prosperity and long-term wealth. By balancing this area of the home you will encourage financial security for you and your family. Don't overdo the money plants and Chinese three-legged money-toad ornaments, though, as too many cures can create havoc with your finances. Alternatively, they may improve your prospects and increase your wealth but generate other problems. Greed, financial manipulation, and envy are likely to take over if you get too obsessed with boosting this area of your home. Note that a bathroom in the southeast corner of your home can be detrimental to your finances, as the positive energy will be constantly flushed away. If you have a bathroom in this area, it's best to keep the toilet seat down and the door shut when the room is not in use. To harmonize the southeast further, incorporate a fire (bright lighting and red glass objects) and water (a small aquarium or images of fish) cure.

EAST: FAMILY AND WELL-BEING

Key element: The eastern sector of your home is reinforced by wood enhancements.

To improve the general health and well-being of your family or to improve family relationships, place objects such as plants, natural wooden objects, an ornamental jade tree, or a piece of malachite in this part of the home.

Harmony in the East Sector

We all know that good health is the key to a happy life, so it's important to focus on balancing the energy of this area well. If you have a missing east sector due to the shape of your home, it's imperative that you hang a mirror facing directly eastward to encourage and reflect positive energy. Also use cures and enhancements in the eastern corners of every room to reinforce this missing area.

The Chinese believe good health is about the balance of yin (cold) and yang (hot) energy in the body, while allowing the Ch'i to flow freely. In Feng Shui, it's important to use wood cures in tandem with water and fire to get the balance of energy right. Plants are essential, but don't fill your eastern sector with twenty spider plants and expect to be as fit as a fiddle. Boost the east with a water feature such as a painting or other images of ships, waves, and waterfalls. The water or the image of water must be active and in motion for this enhancement to be highly beneficial. Avoid scenes of lakes and ponds, as they can create depressing rather than vitalizing energy. Replace any withered plants immediately. If you have no room for potted plants, then incorporate a painting of a vase of flowers or peaches (a Chinese symbol of longevity).

WEST: CHILDREN AND CREATIVITY

Key element: The west sector of your home is reinforced with metal enhancements.

To promote creativity and fertility, whether your goal is to create children of the mind, soul, or body, place a set of wind chimes, a brass bell, or a white, gold, or silver image in this part of your home.

Harmony in the West Sector

We all want to have happy, healthy children, and by activating and balancing the west part of your home, you will create a harmonious family life and boost the psyches and development of your children. This is also an important area for your own creativity and fertility. Like anything in Feng Shui, however, if you use too much metal enhancement you'll end up with obstinate, uncontrollable children with academic problems. You might also find that too much metal enhancement affects your fertility if you're hoping to have children, or that your creative juices stop flowing when you're trying to finish that novel. To reinforce good energy here, incorporate earth and water cures to bring balance to the area. A good earth booster for this part of your home is a piece of pink tourmaline or rose quartz crystal. To motivate a child, place a piece of amethyst crystal in the child's work area. Introduce ceramic, glassware, or objets d'art. Fill a basket or jar with pebbles or shells from the beach.

SOUTHWEST: RELATIONSHIPS AND LOVE

Key element: The southwest area of your home is reinforced using earth enhancements.

To enhance love, bring new romance, or make relationships more enduring, use pairs of real flowers (fresh ones are best), an illustration of a pair of lovebirds or mandarin ducks, or figurines of couples (but not all of these at once!). A piece of rose quartz crystal helps generate tolerance and under-standing.

Harmony in the Southwest Sector

The southwest corner of your home is usually bright and well lit by natural light. This is a crucial area to work on if you want harmonious love relationships or new romance. It doesn't help to balance the area if you cram it with endless photos of you and your partner. It also doesn't help the situation if you put lots of pictures of you on your own or keep a hoard of old letters, mementos, or souvenirs from past love affairs in this area. Too much earth enhancement in the southwest area will swamp you with love problems rather than create harmony, so you should incorporate several fire and metal cures to balance the more self-indulgent aspects of earth with passion and integrity. Incorporate a piece of metal fur-niture or gilt picture frames to add metal.

If the southwest area is your bedroom, don't hang mirrors that reflect the bed, as this distorts physical desire and also causes bad sleeping patterns. Introduce some fire by adding shades of red to the fabrics or décor; for a metal enhancement, choose a brass or wrought-iron bedstead.

NORTHEAST: EDUCATION AND KNOWLEDGE

Key element: The northeast area of your home is reinforced using earth enhancements.

To improve self-wisdom, pass school exams, or help with educational issues, fill a bowl with small stones or pebbles and place it on a ledge or table. Use soft ochre colors, or place images of harvests, autumn, or a favorite landscape on the walls.

Harmony in the Northeast Sector

To maintain the balance in this part of your home, it's essential that you place fire cures here. Too much earth enhancement can make family members show off their knowledge and believe they know best or use their educational achievements as power-tripping or manipulative tools. To activate a good sense of achievement and educational success, use red in your décor or hang up a gilt-framed mirror. If this area falls in your study, then it's doubly auspicious, but you need to balance this high-powered energy with a metal cure, too. For example, line drawings, etchings, or engravings on the wall promote good metal energy. In the northeast corner of the room in which you study, place an amethyst crystal to boost the power of the mind.

NORTHWEST: COMMUNICATION, FRIENDS, MENTORS

Key element: The northwest area of your home is reinforced using metal enhancements.

To improve your relationships with friends, colleagues, and mentors and to open the communication channels for new contacts or beneficial advice, use the color white, or place silver-threaded cushions or wind chimes in this area.

Harmony in the Northwest Sector

This sector of your home is revered above all the others in traditional Feng Shui. The Chinese considered this to be an area associated with good luck. "Mentor luck," as they call it, forms the key to success and good fortune. Having a mentor was regarded as the pathway to power and ultimate happiness. To attract this kind of luck and cultivate mentors (or simply people who can get you where you want to be), you must balance this area really well. If you place too heavy an emphasis on metal cures, however, your networking system will be overloaded with "unlucky" mentors. In other words, you may become desperate to meet the right contact and end up listening to everyone you meet. Alternatively, you may scare off the real mentors rather than drawing them to you. The addition of earth cures will give you every opportunity for good communication and networking. Incorporate natural crystals or ceramic ornaments, and use earth colors such as ochres and yellows in your soft furnishings or décor to complement white walls.

CENTER: THE CORE

Key element: For the core area, there is no ruling element, so use a combination of all the elements.

Choose one enhancement from each of the elements to enhance self-love and personal growth.

If the core area falls in a part of your house where several walls meet, as is often the case, use images on the walls rather than trying to place objects in awkward positions. If the core area falls in the middle of a room or in a hallway, then use the cures on the nearest table, ledge, or wall.

For example:

To add wood:
Choose a favorite upright plant or a vibrant landscape image.

To add fire:
Place a mirror on the wall facing good light.

To add water:
Place a piece of aquamarine on a shelf or opt for an image of flowing water.

To add metal:
Place a piece of black obsidian on a low ledge, or coins in a metal cup.

To add earth:
Put a large conch shell on a table, hang a small tapestry, or incorporate soft browns and ochres into your décor.

The more you look into Chinese systems, the more you will discover certain areas of logic that are hard for many people in the West to understand. For example, you'll come upon a Bagua design that makes little sense because it shows one wood, fire, metal, and water sector and three earth sectors that are somewhat weirdly displayed. If you look into other systems, you will discover that the seasons of the year have extra earth months tucked between them. For the time being, we have to accept that there are reasons for this, and look more deeply into these things some other time.

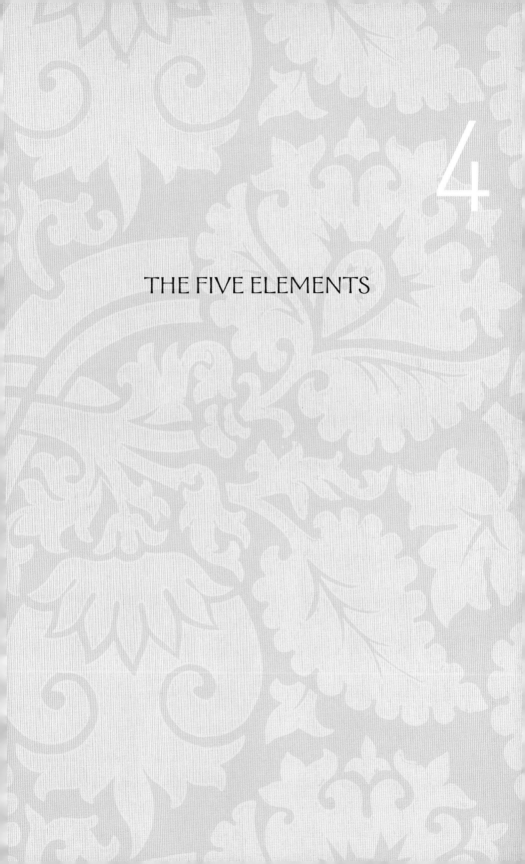

4

THE FIVE ELEMENTS

Most people know there are twelve animal signs in Chinese astrology: the Rat, Ox, Tiger, Rabbit, Dragon, Snake, Horse, Sheep, Monkey, Rooster, Dog and Boar.

Chinese astrological animals.

There are also five elements, corresponding to different energies in Chinese astrology and Feng Shui. These five elements are used to figure out anything from your birth chart to the siting of a house. At this point we've discussed using these elements and their associated cures to boost and harmonize the energy of each aspiration of the Bagua and its corresponding area in the home.

These five elements represent the kind of Ch'i that exists throughout the environment and that works in tandem with the yin and yang qualities and the Bagua energies. As I suggested in the previous chapter, you should use fire cures in the south area of your house because that is where the fire energy is naturally at home. Each of the five elements corresponds to one of the areas of the Bagua. This elemental system is based on the Chinese cycle of creation and destruction.

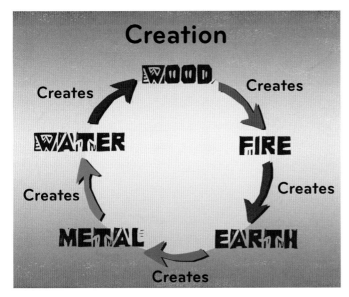

Creation cycle.

According to the Chinese creation cycle, wood can be burned to create fire. Fire burns down to ashes, which create earth. Metal is created within the earth, which creates water, which allows trees to grow and thus creates wood.

Quick List

Wood creates fire, fire creates earth, earth creates metal, metal creates water, and water creates wood.

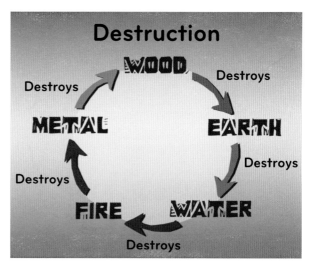

Destruction cycle.

According to the Chinese destruction cycle, wood uses earth to grow, and earth pollutes water. Water douses fire, and fire melts metal, but metal can cut and destroy wood.

Quick List

Wood destroys earth, earth destroys water, water destroys fire, fire destroys metal, and metal destroys wood.

So, for example, because metal destroys wood, metal and wood are not compatible.

When we use cures or enhancements in the home, they have to be compatible with the element that we are treating. For example, if we are working on a wood area, we reinforce it with water cures because water encourages the wood energy, but we wouldn't use water cures to reinforce a fire area, as this would only put out the flames!

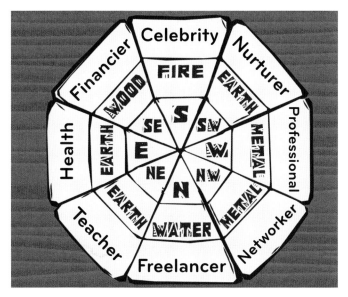

The Bagua, too, is part of this process, and the illustration of the compass shows how all these elements, compass points, and signs interact and work together.

The five elements form a cycle of energy that needs to be harmonized in your environment. For example, if you want to boost the fire sector of your home, you can draw on the other two elements that complement fire, wood and earth. Just don't overload the areas of the home where the energy is naturally resonating with that element. In other words, don't overload the fire corner of your home with too many fire cures; add a little wood and earth to complement and boost the natural fire energy instead.

Elements That Complement Each Other

- Fire can benefit from wood and earth cures.

- Earth can benefit from metal and fire cures.

- Metal can benefit from water and earth cures.

- Water can benefit from wood and metal cures.

- Wood can benefit from fire and water cures.

THE ELEMENTS AND THEIR CURES

The following sections describe how you can use the elements to cure an area of your home that needs to be brought into balance.

The Element of Fire

Here are some examples of fire cures:

- Red or orange paint
- Red lightbulbs (for the brave)
- A picture of a phoenix
- Mirrors
- Candles
- Incense
- Real fires
- Prisms
- Bells
- Spices
- Cacti
- Fireworks images
- Illustrations of battleships
- Illustrations of bonfires
- Red glassware

The Element of Wood

Here are some examples of wood cures:

- Books
- Plants
- Wooden sculpture
- Green things
- Herbs
- Sage
- Pictures of spring
  meadows
- Olive green
- Gnarled wood
- Oil paintings
- Grasses
- Dried seedpods
- Origami
- Ladders
- Vegetables

✗The Element of Earth

Here are some examples of earth cures:

- Stones
- Pebbles
- Rock crystal
- Yellow objects
- Brown items
- Terra cotta colors
- Antiques
- Shells
- Fossils
- Sponges
- Loofahs
- Glass ornaments
  and jars
- Tapestries
- Soap
- Coffee

The Element of Water

Here are some examples of water cures:

- Fish tank
- Dark blue and black items
- Music
- Illustrations of rivers
- Stones and rocks from the sea
- Coral
- The colors violet and purple
- Sea paintings
- Pictures of pirates
- Illustrations of shipwrecks
- Pictures of ships
- Pictures of boats
- Images of cliffs and waves
- Amber

✕ The Element of Metal

Here are some examples of metal cures:

- Gold leaf
- Gold paint
- Silver
- Stainless steel
- Wrought iron
- White metal objects
- Photography, black-and-white images
- Gilt frames
- Brass rubbings
- Silver threads
- Gold-colored fabric
- White lilies

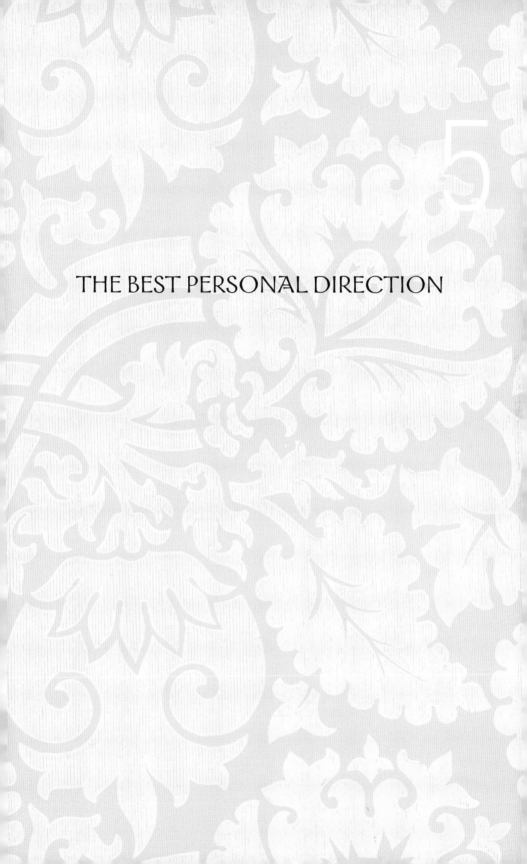

THE BEST PERSONAL DIRECTION

Now that you know how the elements, Bagua, and yin and yang all work together to balance and harmonize the energy of your home, you also need to discover your own most auspicious direction; this is done by determining your *kua* number. This number is your lucky number in Chinese astrology. It tells you which of the eight Bagua compass points is right for you. This is the direction you should face when doing certain things, like sleeping, studying, and even eating.

Here are the steps to figuring out your *kua* number.

FOR THOSE BORN AROUND THE CHINESE NEW YEAR

If you were born between January 1 and February 20, check the Chinese Lunar Calendar to see what date the Chinese New Year fell on in the year of your birth. If you were born *before* the Chinese New Year, you must subtract one from the year of your birth. For example, if you were born on January 23, 1971 (the Chinese New Year in 1971 fell on January 27), you would count your birth year as 1970.

DATES OF THE CHINESE NEW YEAR

January 30, 1930	February 8, 1959	February 17, 1988
February 17, 1931	January 28, 1960	February 6, 1989
February 6, 1932	February 15, 1961	January 27, 1990
January 26, 1933	February 5, 1962	February 15, 1991
February 14, 1934	January 25, 1963	February 4, 1992
February 4, 1935	February 13, 1964	January 23, 1993
January 24, 1936	February 2, 1965	February 10, 1994
February 11, 1937	January 21, 1966	January 31, 1995
January 31, 1938	February 9, 1967	February 19, 1996
February 19, 1939	January 30, 1968	February 7, 1997
February 8, 1940	February 17, 1969	January 28, 1998
January 27, 1941	February 6, 1970	February 16, 1999
February 15, 1942	January 27, 1971	February 5, 2000
February 5, 1943	February 15, 1972	January 24, 2001
January 25, 1944	February 3, 1973	February 12, 2002
February 13, 1945	January 23, 1974	February 1, 2003
February 2, 1946	February 11, 1975	January 21, 2004
January 22, 1947	January 31, 1976	February 9, 2005
February 10, 1948	February 18, 1977	January 29, 2006
January 29, 1949	February 7, 1978	February 18, 2007
February 17, 1950	January 28, 1979	February 7, 2008
February 6, 1951	February 16, 1980	January 26, 2009
January 27, 1952	February 5, 1981	February 17, 2010
February 14, 1953	January 25, 1982	February 3, 2011
February 3, 1954	February 13, 1983	January 23, 2012
January 24, 1955	February 2, 1984	February 10, 2013
February 12, 1956	February 20, 1985	January 31, 2014
January 31, 1957	February 9, 1986	February 19, 2015
February 18, 1958	January 29, 1987	

THE CALCULATION

1. Take the last two digits of your birth year and add them together. For example, if you were born in 1970, then you'd add 7 and 0, to equal 7. If the result is greater than 9, add the two digits together to get a final result of a single digit.

2. If you're female, add 5 to the number that you have produced. For example, 5 + 7 = 12.

3. If you're male, subtract your answer from 10. For example, 10 − 7 = 3.

4. If the number you end up with is greater than 9 (as in the female example, above) add the two digits together and reduce them to 1. For example: 1 + 2 = 3.

5. If the answer is 5 and you are male, your most auspicious direction is the same as it is for number 2.

6. If the answer is 5 and you are female, your most auspicious direction is the same as for number 8.

Example 1

1. Warren was born on January 17, 1984.

2. The Chinese New Year was February 2 in that year, so he has to move his year of birth back to 1983.

3. He adds the last two digits of his year together: 8 + 3 = 11.

4. He must now reduce this to one number: 1 + 1 = 2.

5. He now takes 2 away from 10: 10 − 2 = 8.

6. Warren's *kua* number is 8.

Example 2

1. Darcy was born on September 28, 1987.

2. She must add the last two digits of her year together: $8 + 7 = 15$.

3. She must now reduce this to one number: $1 + 5 = 6$.

4. She must now add 5 to the number: $5 + 6 = 11$.

5. She must now reduce this to one number: $1 + 1 = 2$.

6. Darcy's *kua* number is 2.

KUA BEST DIRECTIONS

1. Southeast
2. Northeast
3. South
4. North
5. (Male) Northeast
   (Female) Southwest

6. West
7. Northwest
8. Southwest
9. East

Although the Bagua locations of your home are fixed, it is useful to know the best direction for you to face when working, sitting for long periods of time, eating, and sleeping. So if your best direction is east, try to have the headboard of your bed facing east. When relaxing in your living space, eating in a restaurant, or signing an important document, try to sit facing east. Your best direction reinforces your personal energy and is highly auspicious for balancing the other energies in the environment.

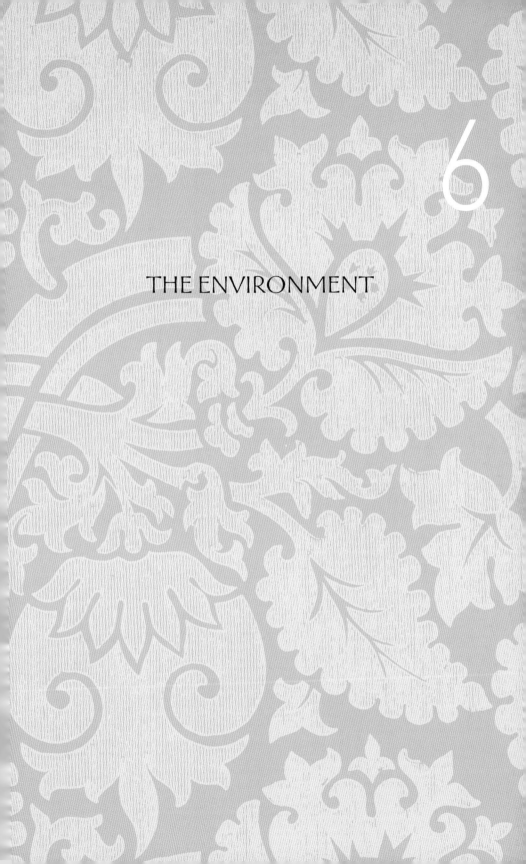

6

THE ENVIRONMENT

Apart from the inside of the home, in traditional Feng Shui, the outside—particularly the sector in front of your main entrance—is very important. This area is called the "redbird," and it is highly auspicious.

First of all, is your house, room, or apartment at the end of a cul-de-sac?

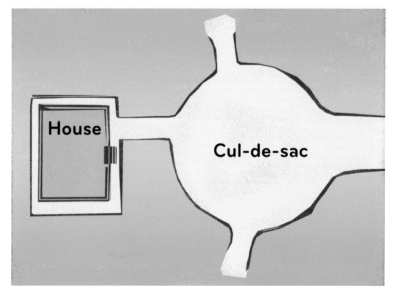

A house at the end of a cul-de-sac is in an inauspicious position. You should instigate a cure.

Second, do you have a road, street, or path pointing directly toward your home? You might live in an apartment at the end of a corridor or your house might be positioned on a sharp bend of a road. The energy directed straight down the road toward you is highly inauspicious. Energy that can come toward you in a straight line is called a "secret arrow," and secret arrows are best kept away from your home.

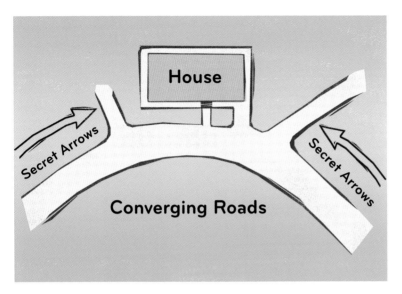

This house is also vulnerable to secret-arrow energy.

The cures for secret-arrow energy are simple. Place wind chimes in front of the main entrance, put plants at either side of your doorway to create spirals of Ch'i, or if you have enough room, put a small fountain or trickling water feature near the front entrance. All these cures generate a good flow of positive Ch'i.

GARDENS

- If you have a garden, is it in good shape?
- Is it tidy and clear of trash, or is it overgrown and messy?
- Does the path meander to the front door, or does it come straight off the road via steps?

Most people who live in an urban area have straight paths. A simple remedy is to hang baskets of flowers or to place standing pots of plants on either side of the entrance. Clear away any trash. If you're always putting off the cleaning up, an interesting point to ponder is whether you could also be making excuses about cleaning up your own life.

Plants breaking up the line of a straight path.

Garden Dos and Don'ts

The art of good Feng Shui in the garden is to ensure that everything flows and meanders. Straight paths, rigid or formal geometrical beds of flowers, and lifeless empty patios and terraces don't generate good Ch'i. Foliage plants are yin, while big stones and boulders are yang. Both can be incorporated into a garden, but they should always be in balance with each other. You can introduce curvy lines and patterns by using subtly different colors or types of plant.

Think carefully about your fences and walls. Sometimes high fences make good screens against secret arrows. If you can see telegraph poles or groups of towers from your home, then add trelliswork or grow a vine across the terrace to block off and deflect the secret-arrow energy away from your home.

Create a trellis across your terrace in the garden to deflect secret-arrow energy.

A meandering stream provides very beneficial energy; ponds can be set into a small garden as well, but you must ensure that the water doesn't stagnate, so add a fountain in the center or some kind of water feature to keep the pond flowing. Flowing water collects and disperses Ch'i. If you opt for a pond, introduce some fish; the best combination is said to be eight red or golden fish plus one black fish to balance the others. Never have an even number of fish; that is considered inauspicious. While flowing water is nice, it can be impractical in small gardens and tiny city spaces, but curvy paths and edging around lawns can take their place.

If you don't have a garden and you live in an apartment at the end of a long corridor, hang wind chimes outside your door. Alternatively, hang a Bagua mirror (an octagonal mirror found in most New Age shops) on the outside of the door, with the mirror facing out.

You can also apply the Bagua system to the garden, just as you do to the home. Draw a plan of your garden, place the Bagua drawing over the garden, and align the directions so that north on the drawing lines up with north on the Bagua.

For example, to make the most of your love life, boost the southwest corner of your garden with climbing red roses or a yang feature such as a garden sculpture.

IS YOUR HOUSE AN EAST OR WEST HOME?

According to Feng Shui, there are two types of houses and similarly two groups of people who are known as the east and west groups. Following is a quick way of determining which is the overall best direction for your house to face. This is most useful to know if you are thinking of building your own house or if you are moving somewhere new. If you choose a house that is basically aligned in the same direction as your group, then obviously you will benefit from that affinity. However, if you live with several members of a family or if you have a partner, there may be conflicting directions.

East-group people feel more comfortable in east-group houses, and west-group people feel more comfortable in west-group houses.

Whether you are east group or west group depends on your *kua* number, as shown below.

Kua Number Group

1. East
2. West
3. East
4. East
5. (Male) West

   (Female) West
6. West
7. West
8. West
9. East

- Homes are classed as east houses if their front doors face southeast, northeast, southwest, or east.
- Homes are classed as west houses if their front doors face north, south, west or northwest.

What we are trying to discover here is whether the house is in a good direction generally for you. If one of your family is east and everyone else is west, then the people most compatible with the house will get the most benefit from the Feng Shui cures. But that doesn't mean the odd one out is going to have problems; all you need to do is to reinforce his or her own element in the room where he or she sleeps.

HARMONIZING CH'I IN THE HOME

By now you have decluttered your home, done some space clearing, checked the outside of your house, and found the Bagua sectors that relate to the different areas of your home. You might also have already added some cures to reinforce specific themes in your life. Next you need to attend to the whole of the home by maximizing the harmonious energy of each room.

THE FRONT DOOR

The front door is one of the most important places to work with, simply because this is the main entrance for the Ch'i to come into your home. Ideally, the front door should face the favorable direction of the person who is the head of the household. Favorable directions can be found according to your *kua* number. If the front door doesn't face this direction, don't panic. The most important thing is to check the energy or influences that are outside the home. For example, if secret-arrow energy is pointing at the entrance to your home, hang a Bagua mirror on the front door to deflect the difficult energy.

A satellite dish generates secret-arrow energy.

Examples of Bad Front-Door Directions

- A straight path and large tree threaten the home.
- A satellite dish opposite the home generates secret-arrow energy.
- High-rise buildings distribute negative energy in your direction.

Examples of Good Front-Door Directions

- A small water feature near the front door is beneficial.
- A curved path is better than a straight one.
- A low wall or hedge helps circulate Ch'i.

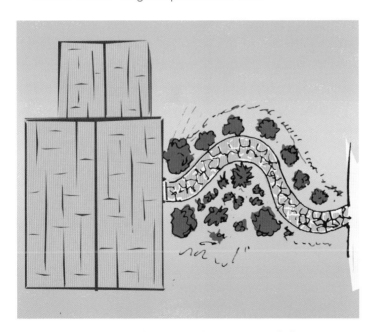

A curved path is better than a straight one.

ENTRANCES

What is your entrance like? Do you have a front hall, or does the front entrance lead straight into the living area? Wherever the first step across the threshold of your home leads, you must always keep the entrance clear and uncluttered. Make sure shoes, coats, books, papers, knickknacks, and letters don't pile up on a hall table. This type of clutter creates stagnant yin energy. If you have space, place a jar or vase of flowers near the entrance to encourage positive, earthy energy to enter the home.

If you can walk through your main entrance and see the back door straight ahead of you, it's important to introduce some plants or wind chimes in the entrance hall to soften the flow of energy. Otherwise, the Ch'i will just flow straight through the house, in one door and out the other. A long corridor is also a very inviting place for secret-arrow energy. Hang a large crystal over the doorway to deflect the straight lines of negative energy.

A plant softening the flow of energy.

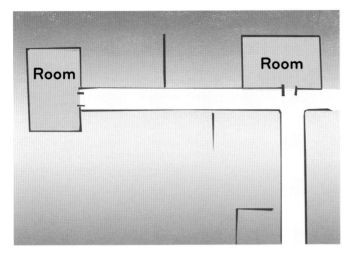

Long corridors invite negative energy.

THE KITCHEN

In traditional Feng Shui, you should never have fire and water together, as they are opposite energies. This can pose a problem in a small kitchen, where the sink is often next to the oven.

Hot ovens = fire; running taps = water.

There's not much you can do to separate them if you have a fitted kitchen. If your oven and sink are close together, the remedy is to place a wood cure either above or between these two difficult energies to harmonize them and bridge the gap between the creative cycle of "water creates wood; wood creates fire." This cure could be something like a small plant on a shelf or a wooden spoon hanging on the wall.

According to ancient Chinese philosophy, the kitchen is one of the most creative areas of the home. This is where life is energized, where food is cooked and the process of creating and blending ingredients is like Feng Shui itself. Most of us can't get excited by day-to-day cooking or shoving a supermarket dinner into the microwave. (By the way, microwaves invoke highly charged yang energy and are worth avoiding if you can).

Check the state of your kitchen now. If it's full of dirty dishes, clean it up, and if there is stale food in the fridge, throw it out. If you're hoping for an improvement in your love life or life in general, then the sooner you create the right ambience in the kitchen, which is the heart of the home according to the Chinese, the sooner your own heart will be harmonized.

Here are some harmonizing tips for a healthy and creative kitchen and for sustaining happy relationships.

Tips

Ovens should face the strongest source of natural light. The Chinese believe that bad energy comes from the north, so it's better for the source of all nourishment—the oven and cooking process itself—to face south. If you can't move your oven around, then hang a mirror directly opposite the oven to reflect and maximize natural light. Alternatively, hang a white quartz crystal in the window to reflect bright light all around the room. Just be careful that it isn't likely to direct light onto something that will catch fire.

Is your stove directly opposite the back door? If it is, you might have to move it at some stage. The Chinese always placed their stoves so they could see the back door when

they were cooking, and the same goes for any item of furniture such as a bed, sofa, or easy chair, where you might
be standing or sitting or lying down. Don't turn your back on
a door, because the secret arrows of negative Ch'i will be
drawn to your exposed back. In more primitive times, it was
believed that someone could creep up on you and hurt you
while you were cooking or resting.

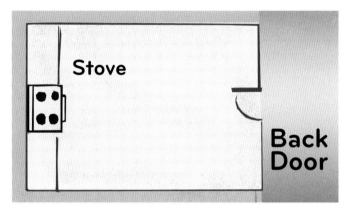

A poor kitchen arrangement: a stove is best
positioned somewhere other than directly
opposite the back door.

White is the favorite color for Chinese kitchens because it
symbolizes purity and promotes good health. Don't store
cutlery in a stagnant area, such as in a corner cupboard or
at the bottom of a cupboard, and make sure your knives and
forks are in a drawer near an entrance, doorway, or window
for positive energy to flow. Finally, a bathroom near a kitchen
produces negative energy, so keep the door closed and the
toilet lid down.

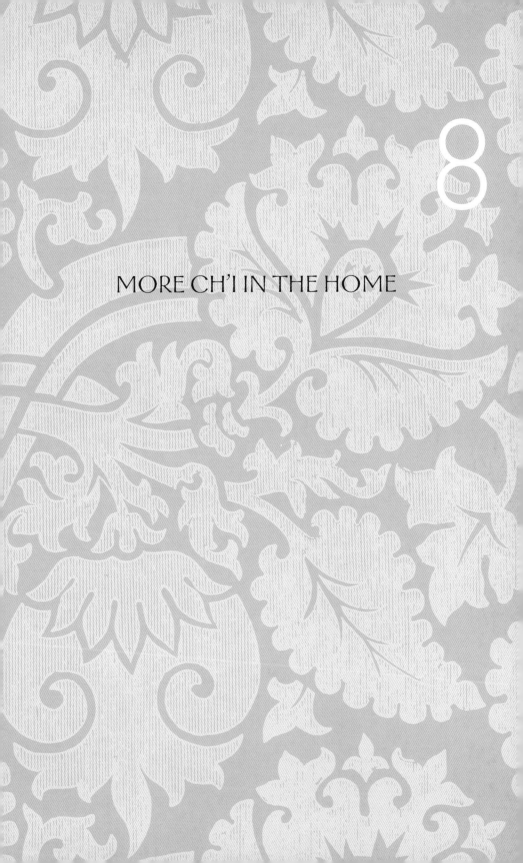

8

MORE CH'I IN THE HOME

THE BATHROOM

Bathrooms and toilets are generally big sources of trouble in Feng Shui. It might not look like it, but you can easily lose your money or your partner if you're not careful. Seriously, this is one room where you can't make major changes without calling in the plumber, so if you think your good energy is being flushed away, make the following adjustments.

As mentioned earlier, always keep the toilet seat down and close the door. Don't put trailing plants on top of the toilet tank or on the floor; this attracts energy downward toward the outflow of water. As bathrooms are very much water areas, even if yours does not fall in the water or north sector of the Bagua, you must harmonize this room with wood and metal cures. For example, hang an image of trees or a wild landscape in the bathroom. Use stainless-steel towel bars or bathroom fittings. Avoid candles in the bathroom. However romantic they seem, the tension between fire energy and water energy can cause problems in your relationships. Soft greens and neutral colors such as soapstone whites and sandstone are excellent wall colors. Choose a white bathroom suite, if you can. If you're stuck with something out-of-date and unfashionable, add dashes of these colors in your bathroom accessories and towels.

THE BEDROOM

The bedroom is highly auspicious for intimate relationships and personal psychic energy, which is restored during a good night's sleep. For obvious reasons, the bed is a potent place for sexual relationships, but it's also where you sleep, dream, and wake up. If your bed is in a bad spot according to the Feng Shui tradition, then you're going to have difficult sleep patterns and problems in your sex life, too.

First, does the foot of the bed point straight toward the doorway? If it does, you are better off moving it to face a different direction, unless of course the head of the bed is located in your personal best direction, in which case hang a small mirror facing the doorway, perhaps on the end of the bed, to deflect any secret-arrow energy coming straight at you. Many people are superstitious about having the bed facing the doorway because secret arrows of maleficent energy can swoop through your door and blaze their way across the bed, leading to a broken relationship as well as broken sleep. Others are superstitious because in days gone by (and probably still today) those who died in their beds were carried out feet first through the doorway.

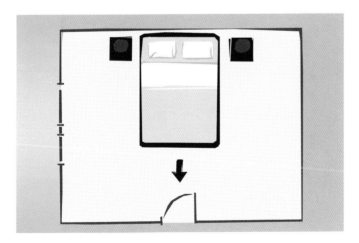

The end of the bed pointing toward the door is inauspicious.

Check the beams or joists over your bedroom. Are you sleep-ing directly under a heavy beam that runs over the bed? If you are, try to move the bed somewhere else. These kinds of "enemy lines" can destroy your sex life, your sleep, and your psychic energy. If you can't move the bed or it just ends up under another beam, be cunning. Choose bedcovers or duvets that have strong patterns of lines positioned at right angles to the beams or joists. This will take the energy along the new lines and off the end or sides of the bed, deflecting and balancing the negative Ch'i.

Poor bedroom arrangement: the bed should be somewhere other than directly under a beam.

Avoid hanging lights directly over the bed. This highly focused yang energy will beam down directly on whichever part of your body the light is above. This can create aches and pains as well as an erratic sex life and sleep pattern. Move the bed or move the light.

Energize and harmonize your bedroom (whether it is in the relationship, or southwest, sector of the Bagua or not) with some metal or fire cures. Place two red candles or red glassware in the bedroom to maximize sexual harmony. A glass pyramid or prism can be an excellent vitalizer if you're single and looking for a partner, or if you want more romance between you and your partner. The power of the pyramid or prism is that, although it has sharp, faceted sides, it directs and attracts energy that may be flowing unevenly. Hang wind chimes outside the window and use mirrors with care. Never hang a mirror facing you when you're in bed; this causes problems with self-value and sexuality.

Never sleep with the bed facing a mirror.

Finally, it is strongly recommended that you don't sleep above an empty space such as a garage, storeroom, or empty basement. This is because there will be stagnant Ch'i underneath you, which acts as a depressant rather than a stimulant.

THE STUDY OR OFFICE

Traditionalists believe that the best place to have a study or office is in the northwest area of your home, as this sector encourages good contacts, interaction, and lucky breaks. If you can't manage to locate your workplace here, however, strategically place some metal and earth cures around the place you work or study. Metal cures include stainless-steel office accessories, hollow-metal wind chimes, or a landscape painting. Earth cures include natural objects such as a bowl of stones or shells; put fresh flowers in the east corner of the study or office space for yang energy, and position a small plant in the southeast of the study or office space to enhance your prospects. Use a white quartz crystal on your desk's southwest corner to improve business relationships.

If you can place your desk so it's facing your best personal direction, so much the better, and leave the area in front of your desk free of clutter. Try to ensure that you can see the door from the desk, rather than having your back to it. Having your back to the door is not only inauspicious, but can actually make you feel uncomfortable. The arrangement that I have suggested allows the Ch'i to circulate and create a sense of welcome into your space.

Keep your space as free of clutter as possible. Put files and books away rather than leaving them lying all over the desk or floor. Clutter like this creates too much yin energy and stagnant Ch'i. If you have lots of sharp furniture edges, from chairs and tables to desks and filing cabinets, add more earth cures such as wall paints in terra cotta or yellow ochre, leather chairs, or a tapestry on the wall.

THE DINING ROOM OR DINING AREA

Use soft colors and lighting in the dining area. The ideal shape for a table is an octagon, but not many people find this practical or, for that matter, easy to find. The next best thing is a round table because that shape symbolizes creativity and completion. If you have a square or rectangular table, use circular place mats or place a round bowl of fruit in the center of the table to compensate for the square shape and to add balance. A mirror on the wall that reflects the abundance of food on the table will also reflect the abundance you will have in your life.

Dining Room
Mirror
Even Number of Chairs

A good dining room arrangement: note the even number of chairs around the table.

Ensure that chairs and tables don't obstruct doorways, and always have an even number of chairs set out. Even if you're expecting only three people, set out four chairs because even numbers are more balancing than uneven numbers.

THE LIVING ROOM

The living room is probably the place in which you spend most of your time, apart from the bedroom or the kitchen. It is often the most important room in the home because it's where we "show off" who we are. We invite strangers into this part of the home, and it really does expose who we actually are. First impressions last a long time, and some impressions can be negative. For instance, you have probably had the experience of feeling uncomfortable in other people's living spaces because they have very different lifestyles and needs from yours. It is quite possible for others to feel uncomfortable in *your* living area, so try to remain objective about it. A living area is exactly what it says it is. It lives and breathes a message of who you are and is the essence of your personality.

Always have sofas facing a window or doorway. Don't have any seats with their backs facing a door unless you really can't help it. If you can't face or see a doorway from a seating area, hang a mirror so you can see the door when you are seated. Keep the center of the living room empty so that friends and strangers alike can move through this space without disrupting the energy flow that circulates around the room.

Furniture should include curves and soft furnishings. Choose warm and welcoming colors, such as soft pastels, sage greens, apricots, or palest pink. Always keep a piece of white quartz crystal in the south sector of the living room to enhance other people's appreciation of and respect for your personal style and taste. This is the room where you will create success in your life, even if it isn't in the south area of your home. If you don't have an open fire or even a false fire or hearth, place four large candles in a special place to create an alternate type of fire centerpiece for your home. This is highly beneficial energy in the living room to promote success in all you do.

A fireplace creates a cozy atmosphere.

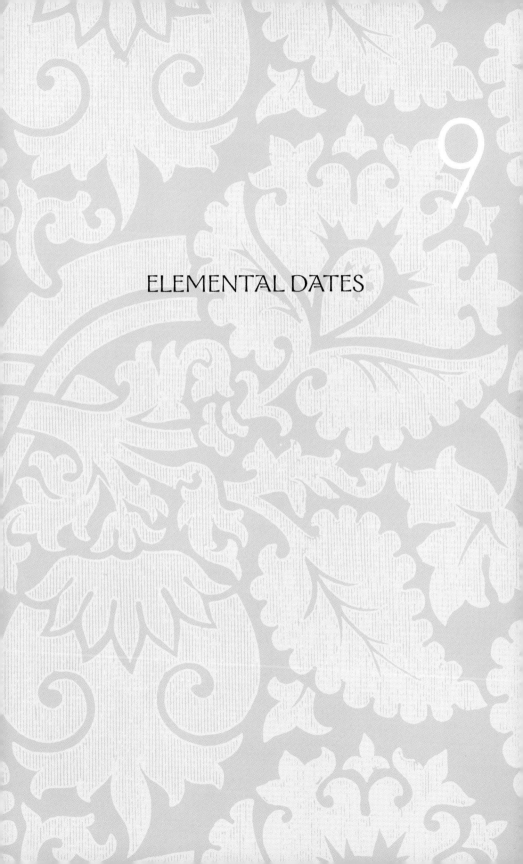

9

ELEMENTAL DATES

In Chinese astrology and in Feng Shui, the five elements are reflective of the energies within us as individuals. Harmonious relationships depend on activating your own personal element within the environment, so the cures you should use are usually ones that balance or enhance the energies that may be missing. Using too much of your own element will create problems, however, so you must boost your own element subtly.

While each new year brings in a new animal sign, each element runs for two years at a time, so we can have Wood/Rat followed by Wood/Ox, then Fire/Tiger followed by Fire/Rabbit. Over the course of sixty years, each element will link with each sign, and then the whole sequence begins again. Consult the list below to discover your birth element.

LIST OF ELEMENTAL BIRTH YEARS

Year			Element
January 30, 1930	–	February 16, 1931	Metal, yang
February 17, 1931	–	February 5, 1932	Metal, yin
February 6, 1932	–	January 25, 1933	Water, yang
January 26, 1933	–	February 13, 1934	Water, yin
February 14, 1934	–	February 3, 1935	Wood, yang
February 4, 1935	–	January 23, 1936	Wood, yin
January 24, 1936	–	February 10, 1937	Fire, yang
February 11, 1937	–	January 30, 1938	Fire, yin
January 31, 1938	–	February 18, 1939	Earth, yang
February 19, 1939	–	February 7, 1940	Earth, yin
February 8, 1940	–	January 26, 1941	Metal, yang

Year			Element
January 27, 1941	–	February 14, 1942	Metal, yin
February 15, 1942	–	February 4, 1943	Water, yang
February 5, 1943	–	January 24, 1944	Water, yin
January 25, 1944	–	February 12, 1945	Wood, yang
February 13, 1945	–	February 1, 1946	Wood, yin
February 2, 1946	–	January 21, 1947	Fire, yang
January 22, 1947	–	February 9, 1948	Fire, yin
February 10, 1948	–	January 28, 1949	Earth, yang
January 29, 1949	–	February 16, 1950	Earth, yin
February 17, 1950	–	February 5, 1951	Metal, yang
February 6, 1951	–	January 26, 1952	Metal, yin
January 27, 1952	–	February 13, 1953	Water, yang
February 14, 1953	–	February 2, 1954	Water, yin
February 3, 1954	–	January 23, 1955	Wood, yang
January 24, 1955	–	February 11, 1956	Wood, yin
February 12, 1956	–	January 30, 1957	Fire, yang
January 31, 1957	–	February 17, 1958	Fire, yin
February 18, 1958	–	February 7, 1959	Earth, yang
February 8, 1959	–	January 27, 1960	Earth, yin
January 28, 1960	–	February 14, 1961	Metal, yang
February 15, 1961	–	February 4, 1962	Metal, yin
February 5, 1962	–	January 24, 1963	Water, yang
January 25, 1963	–	February 12, 1964	Water, yin
February 13, 1964	–	February 1, 1965	Wood, yang
February 2, 1965	–	January 20, 1966	Wood, yin
January 21, 1966	–	February 8, 1967	Fire, yang
February 9, 1967	–	January 29, 1968	Fire, yin
January 30, 1968	–	February 16, 1969	Earth, yang
February 17, 1969	–	February 5, 1970	Earth, yin
February 6, 1970	–	January 26, 1971	Metal, yang

Year			Element
January 27, 1971	–	February 14, 1972	Metal, yin
February 15, 1972	–	February 2, 1973	Water, yang
February 3, 1973	–	January 22, 1974	Water, yin
January 23, 1974	–	February 10, 1975	Wood, yang
February 11, 1975	–	January 30, 1976	Wood, yin
January 31, 1976	–	February 17, 1977	Fire, yang
February 18, 1977	–	February 6, 1978	Fire, yin
February 7, 1978	–	January 27, 1979	Earth, yang
January 28, 1979	–	February 15, 1980	Earth, yin
February 16, 1980	–	February 4, 1981	Metal, yang
February 5, 1981	–	January 24, 1982	Metal, yin
January 25, 1982	–	February 12, 1983	Water, yang
February 13, 1983	–	February 1, 1984	Water, yin
February 2, 1984	–	February 19, 1985	Wood, yang
February 20, 1985	–	February 8, 1986	Wood, yin
February 9, 1986	–	January 28, 1987	Fire, yang
January 29, 1987	–	February 16, 1988	Fire, yin
February 17, 1988	–	February 5, 1989	Earth, yang
February 6, 1989	–	January 26, 1990	Earth, yin
January 27, 1990	–	February 14, 1991	Metal, yang
February 15, 1991	–	February 3, 1992	Metal, yin
February 4, 1992	–	January 22, 1993	Water, yang
January 23, 1993	–	February 9, 1994	Water, yin
February 10, 1994	–	January 30, 1995	Wood, yang
January 31, 1995	–	February 18, 1996	Wood, yin
February 19, 1996	–	February 6, 1997	Fire, yang
February 7, 1997	–	January 27, 1998	Fire, yin
January 28, 1998	–	February 15, 1999	Earth, yang
February 16, 1999	–	February 4, 2000	Earth, yin
February 5, 2000	–	January 23, 2001	Metal, yang
January 24, 2001	–	February 11, 2002	Metal, yin

elemental dates

February 12, 2002 – January 31, 2003	Water, yang
February 1, 2003 – January 21, 2004	Water, yin
January 22, 2004 – February 8, 2005	Wood, yang
February 9, 2005 – January 28, 2006	Wood, yin
January 29, 2006 – February 17, 2007	Fire, yang
February 18, 2007 – February 6, 2008	Fire, yin
February 7, 2008 – January 25, 2009	Earth, yang
January 26, 2009 – February 13, 2010	Earth, yin
February 14, 2010 – February 2, 2011	Metal, yang
February 3, 2011 – January 22, 2012	Metal, yin
January 23, 2012 – February 9, 2013	Water, yang
February 10, 2013 – January 30, 2014	Water, yin
January 31, 2014 – February 18, 2015	Wood, yang

10

THE FIVE ELEMENTAL
PERSONALITY TYPES

In Feng Shui it's important to reinforce your own elemental energy within your home. This can be complicated if you are part of a large family, yet you can still use your own special corner of a room and personalize it to boost your energy flow. Each member of the family can have one as well. Review your own element's expression, and then create a sacred corner for yourself and for your loved ones. .

Note: If you discover that your family consists of mainly one element—for example, if everyone is fire—then obviously any added fire enhancements would put the home out of balance. In this case, you'd be wise to add harmonious energies via the elements that are compatible with yours.

IF YOU'RE FIRE

You are impulsive and idealistic, and you're enthusiastic about everything you do. With lots of energy to expend, you rarely sit down for long and you need an active lifestyle and busy social life. In love relationships, you need to be the dominant partner and you want exclusive attention in return. Concern with playing the leading role in someone else's life means that you often neglect other people's needs, so it's important to learn to be more compassionate and tolerant in the home. Fire people thrive on friendship and companionship. You have high expectations of loyalty, and you don't take it lightly if someone abuses your friendship or gossips about you behind your back. There's more hope, optimism, and sensitivity in your heart than many people would believe, for all your outgoing impulsiveness. As self-image and self-love take up a lot of your time, you must learn to go with the flow and not try to make others run at your pace. You're passionate about life and love, and you need a partner who can give you the freedom and space that you need.

In Feng Shui, earth and wood cures are the best choices for harmonizing your home and making it compatible with your personality. You produce a lot of energy, and it's buzzy and electric, so too much fire in the home can make your own inner Bagua energies burn out. Expressing anger is healthy, but you need to learn to channel this energy in a positive way, perhaps through sports, dancing, other kinds of physical activity, and healthy debates.

IF YOU'RE EARTH

Reliable and committed, you're likely to be the practical one in the household. You hate change, but when committed to a relationship you'll stick it out through thick and thin, even if it's difficult. Sensuality is a keyword for you. Whether it's the pleasure of food, sex, or just taking a walk through the park, the back-to-nature side of you needs to be expressed and energized. You prefer peace and stability to action and spontaneity, but that doesn't prevent you from being a romantic. Avoiding conflict, you'll do anything for an easy life, but this can get you into trouble because you never express what you truly want. This can lead to growing resentment, either from you or within the home. You can be very possessive, so you need to let your partner have some space. You give out a great deal of warmth, affection, and gentleness, and you expect it from others in return.

In Feng Shui, fire and metal cures will help you to focus on giving true love rather than expecting too much. Too much earth enhancement in the home will make you more controlling, but with the addition of spontaneous fire and the independent nature of metal, you will begin to be easier and more compassionate to yourself, not just good to others.

IF YOU'RE WOOD

Unconventional and intellectual, you need to maintain your independence and you find it hard to live in a family setup unless the family lets you have a lot of personal space and freedom. You have a practical streak, but you'd rather talk about life and love and analyze relationships than get too personal. Love is something that happens in your head rather than your heart. You avoid your feelings, and you prefer a lover or partner who is neither slushy nor sentimental. You thrive best with someone who is very much your equal, but it's hard for anyone to live up to your high ideals. You can cause problems in relationships by refusing to listen to others and stubbornly persisting in your own viewpoint. Friends are more important to you than relatives, and your social life takes up as much time as your work. What you need most is someone who honors your need for freedom but who can still be there for you as a friend.

In Feng Shui, too much wood in your home will make you more opinionated and rebellious, so avoid filling your house with hundreds of potted plants. Reinforce your personal energy with moderation and balance by using water and fire cures.

IF YOU'RE METAL

Competitive and ambitious, you thrive in a conventional relationship and believe that the family and home are very much an expression of your own image and status. In fact, you can get so obsessive about your home that it becomes a show house rather than a real home. There is a very self-reliant and determined aura about you, and it gives you the ability to get ahead in your career and achieve what you set out to do. In love relationships you look for status, prestige, love, and honor in one person, and as this prefect combination is so hard to find, you may prefer to stay single. Your fear of losing love is as great as your desire to find your ideal partner. This is where you compensate in other areas of life by working hard in your career. You may be the epitome of cool, and you may have a casual and unflustered attitude toward relationships. Being serious about life means you sometimes forget to laugh about it, too, but when you do laugh you reveal a wry and very dry sense of humor. You fear intimacy because it reveals your own inner vulnerabilities, but when you do get involved with someone, you usually want to be the boss. Loyal and single-minded, you're unlikely to stray once you find someone who can build your empire with you.

In Feng Shui, too much metal in your home may bring you great success in life, but it will ultimately create friction in love relationships simply because you'll become more ruthless and self-centered. To free yourself from the chain mail around your heart, introduce earth and water cures.

IF YOU'RE WATER

Not only are you idealistic and easily led astray, but you're one of the most romantic and sensitive people around. Although you love to socialize, when you're at home you need plenty of privacy and a room of your own where you can retreat. Unpredictable and elusive, you love to be in love, and it doesn't really matter with whom, as long as you can throw yourself into the magical, out-of-this-world feeling that being in love creates. However, for all your un-focused and almost gullible attitude to love, you never really let anyone into your emotional space, and your constant need for change makes it hard for anyone to understand your chameleon-like moods. You are versatile, spontane-ous, and imaginative, and you have an extraordinary abil-ity to play any role, so you become exactly like the person you're with. This means that you rarely know yourself, and if you don't know who you are, you can bet that your part-ner doesn't have a clue, either. You may have to experience many different relationships before you find your perfect lover. If, however, you find someone who protects and adores you but gives you enough room to be yourself and enough space to feel you haven't committed your entire self, you're likely to stay put.

In Feng Shui, too much water in the home can make you even more changeable, restless, and lost. Introducing a bal-ance of metal and wood cures with subtle nuances of water will help to give you a sense of your own boundaries and your own needs.

Whatever your personal element is, and regardless of the elements of other people who live in your home, keep the center of your home clear of mess. Keeping that area clutter-free will enhance the health and well-being of everyone living there. Keep the center of each room clear as well, if possible. For ornaments that have sharp points or edges, turn them so that the sharp part faces the wall. Keep the bathroom door closed, especially if you or your family don't like keeping the toilet lid down.

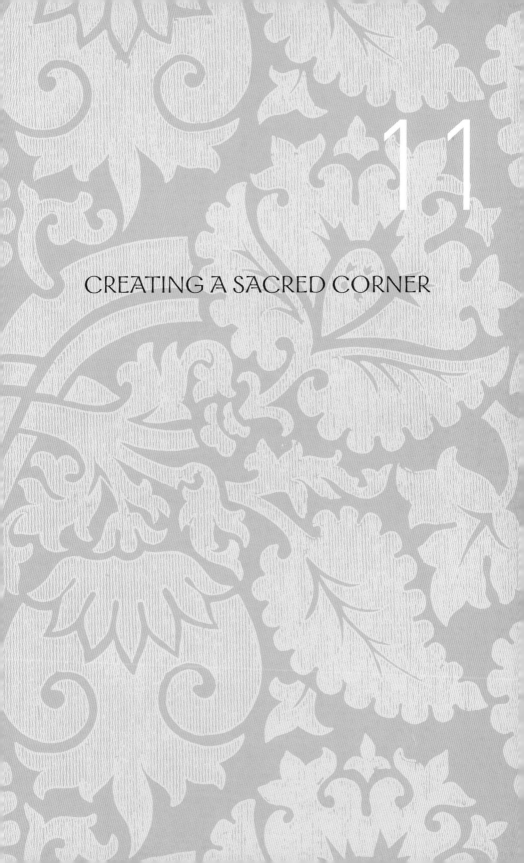

11

CREATING A SACRED CORNER

Whatever element you are identified with, a sacred corner of your own can vitalize your inner energy and help promote harmony and well-being in relationships. Once you have created the space, don't forget to dust it and keep it clear of clutter.

IF YOU'RE FIRE

Be sure to use the south corner of your chosen room and a low surface. Place a small mirror at the back of a low table against the wall and place a single red candle or incense stick in front of the mirror. Place a piece of carnelian or bloodstone next to the candle. Add a painting or photo of poppies or sunflowers. For extra impact, place a prism in your sacred corner to refract and charge every particle of light and energy.

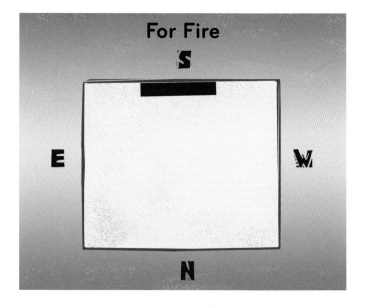

IF YOU'RE EARTH

For the best results, choose the southwest or northeast corner of your chosen room. Try to keep the surface at about shoulder height, and place a small picture of a landscape at the back of the surface. Make sure the surface is covered with a piece of vintage fabric or rich tapestry. Collect some shells or pebbles from a beach or a garden and place them in a small terra cotta bowl, and then put this in front of the images. You can also add a piece of smoky quartz or moonstone for extra harmony.

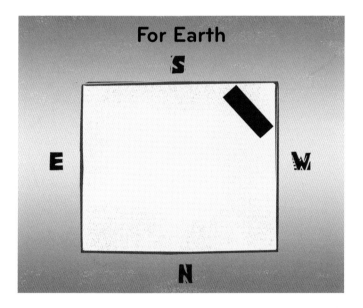

IF YOU'RE WOOD

Make your sacred corner at floor level and ensure that it's in the east or southeast corner of your chosen room. Cover the area with velvet or a rich deep green fabric. Place a wooden sculpture of a bird or green dragon on the fabric (you can find these figures in local or Internet-based Eastern or New Age shops or even in tourist traps). Hang a wooden frame on the wall behind the figures. A book or small spray of dried herbs can be placed to one side of it, and a piece of malachite will make a grand centerpiece and will add to the magical energy.

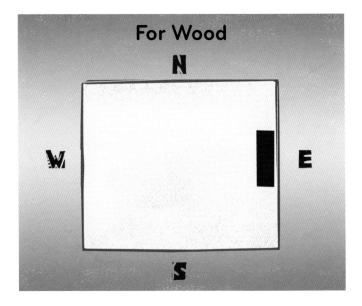

IF YOU'RE WATER

Make sure your sacred place is in the north corner of your chosen room and at about knee height. Cover a ledge or small table with silk or voile in a shade of Prussian blue or aquamarine. Hang up or lean a painting of the sea or a waterfall or any image of moving water against the wall. Place some blue beads in a small glass vessel in the center. Alternatively, use a glass bowl full of marbles. Find a stone cup, fill it with water, and sprinkle it with glitter. Finally, add a piece of amber at the front to give you the deep love connection that you need.

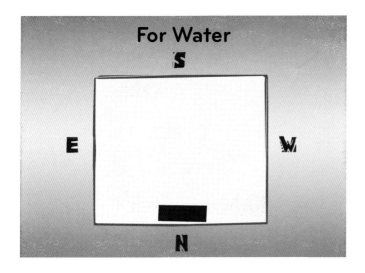

For Water

IF YOU'RE METAL

Choose a surface that is about waist height and in the west or northwest area of your chosen room. Lean or hang a gilt- or silver-framed mirror and place a silver, pewter, or stainless-steel cup in front of the mirror. Alternatively, you might choose to find an old glass and paint it gold. Find a silver necklace and hang it from a metal hook or candle sconce; add a small brass rubbing or etching in the corner. Finally, place a diamond, selenite, or white quartz crystal in the center.

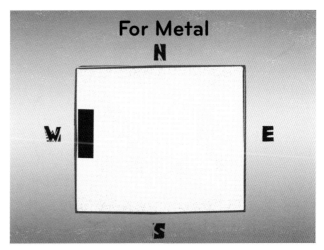

For Metal

✦A WELCOMING SACRED SPACE

Even if you live in the tiniest of studio apartments or share a room, you can easily make a sacred space. In this way, you will welcome whatever you need most into your life. This space is rather like a waiting room—a transitory place where all those who travel take a rest, and then move on. This space will encourage people to travel to your side and will help you to find new pathways and to discover happiness. Create your sacred space near the main entrance to your home.

Simply outline your chosen space in the air with your finger. You can draw an imaginary circle, a figure eight, or any curved shape, as long as it has no sharp angles, which would encourage secret-arrow energy. Of course, you are doing this in only one dimension, but imagine you're doing it in a million dimensions. Once you have traced the outline in the air, purify it with a piece of white quartz crystal left in the room for a day and a night, as this will charge the atmosphere with beneficial energy.

Each time you pass through this space, remind yourself that it's a welcoming space for those who enter your home and for those who have yet to find the pathway to the space in your heart. To confirm that this is your magic space, copy a picture of the talisman on a piece of paper and place it on the wall near the magic space or paint it on the wall as a mural, if you prefer. This is an ancient Taoist talisman for combining good fortune and peace, and it deflects any uneasy or negative energy trying to enter your home.

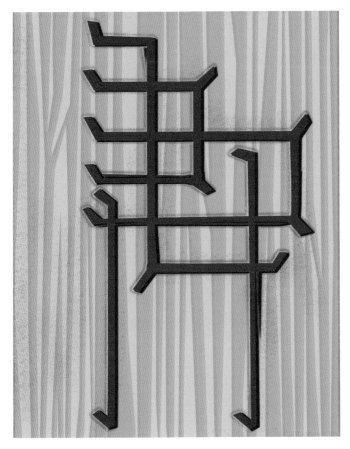

Talisman.

12

RELATIONSHIPS

TO ATTRACT SUCCESS IN LOVE

When people are single, whether by choice or because of circumstances beyond their control, they still want to be in a love relationship, because loving partnerships are an instinctive part of human nature. Every person we meet becomes a signpost that helps us find ourselves and accept who we are as individuals. Feng Shui can help you understand what love means to you. If you create harmony in your home, you will find it easier to understand yourself and to love yourself, and as a result, it will become easier to attract other people into your life who will love you. Understanding your own desires, needs, and values is the way toward healthy relationships. If you're looking for new love, ask yourself the following questions:

1. If you've recently broken up with someone, ask yourself why you split up. What were the motives behind the breakup?

2. If you've never been in an intimate relationship, ask yourself whether you fear commitment or the exposure of your vulnerabilities.

3. Ask whether you have a problem attracting people to yourself.

4. Do you have a problem maintaining a relationship?

5. Do you always pick the wrong types?

6. Why do you think no one will ever be good enough for you?

7. What kind of person are you looking for?

8. Why can't you stop thinking about someone from the past?

THE CURES

The following cures are specifically related to the above questions. Use specific cures for the question or questions that you feel to be most relevant, but be prepared for the situation to change. The kind of love that is important to you now may well change in time, but Feng Shui moves with you and changes with you, just as love can change. Try not to instigate all the cures at once, as this can lead to an overload of energy!

1. Why did you split up?

Use the following cure in the southeast corner of your home so that you can be at peace with yourself. Hang a rose quartz crystal pendant in your window, or place it where natural light will refract its loving qualities around the room.

2. Do you fear commitment?

We fear that if anyone gets too close to us they'll see behind the mask and won't like the real us inside. To project a more confident aura of self-value, place a white quartz crystal in the southeast area of your home. You can also reinforce this cure in the southeast corner of your bedroom.

✗3. Do you have a problem attracting people to you?

Use the following cure as a great source of empowerment. Place either a prism or a red glass bowl or wine goblet in the south corner of your home. Light some incense every evening to reinforce the attraction factor.

4. Do you have a problem maintaining a relationship?

Whatever the reason for losing control of your relationships, use the following cure in the northwest corner of your home. Place four pinecones in a wooden bowl, or you can use a bowl of pine nuts, which are available in delicatessens and supermarkets. Mountain pine symbolizes longevity and commitment in Taoist art, and its effect is considered to be stabilizing and grounding.

5. Do you pick the wrong types?

If you frequently get caught up in this game, then use the following cure in the north corner of your home. Either hang a sodalite pendulum in the window or place a piece of sodalite on the windowsill. Add a small mirror to reflect the crystal's rays during the day and to empower you with responsibility for your choices.

6. Do you believe nobody is good enough for you?

You need to come down to earth. You're probably an idealist with high principles, and you might be so proud of your principles that you are almost narcissistic. What you're actually doing is compensating for your own sense of not being good enough by dumping the problem on everyone you meet. The cure is to place a bonsai tree or plant in the east area of your home to promote more tolerance and compassion for yourself and for others.

x7. What kind of person are you looking for?

This is often the most difficult question to answer, because if you have a problem identifying what you want from a relationship or choosing the kind of partner who will fulfill your needs and love you for being you, you can become completely confused. If this is the case, instigate the following cure. Place a gold or silver ring, a piece of gold-leaf paper, or a silver candlestick in the core area of your home. This will promote integrity and confidence so that you can begin to assert your own needs and discover who you are, and thus the kind of person with whom you would be compatible.

x8. Having problems forgetting someone from your past?

If you can't let go of the past and move on, use the following cure in the west corner of your home. Take two small candles, one white and one black (if you can't get black, then buy the darkest blue you can find), and stand them together in front of a window or mirror. Light both candles. Gradually the black candle will draw away the negative energy and the white candle will invoke clarity and purpose. Once the black candle finally burns out, you will be able to look forward to the future and move on.

13

HARMONIZING LOVE RELATIONSHIPS

If you are currently in a relationship, whether you live with your partner or not, here are some cures and harmonizers to improve your relationship. The choice of cure depends on which elements you both belong to. So, for example, if you are metal and your partner is fire, read the "Metal/Fire" section. All these cures will boost both your romantic and your sexual rapport.

METAL/METAL

The metal/metal relationship is a highly magnetic and sexual attraction that creates a volatile energy in the home. Many battles of will may result from both partners' stubbornness, but you're both ambitious and creative, and you make a powerful team. Remember to honor each other's need for autonomy.

To maintain the passion between you and to increase your chances of joint success, make sure you keep the angles of furniture in your bedroom soft and the lighting subdued. Hang delicate muslin drapes at open windows or around the bed to ensure that the Ch'i moves in curved lines through your personal space. Bring water into your home to encourage ideas to flow easily. Add images of fast-flowing rivers or waterfalls or an aquarium in the southwest corner of your home. For emotional harmony, use calming earth colors such as peach, coral, or camellia to inspire genuine affection and admiration. Sensual bath oils and spicy perfumes will maximize your other senses, too.

METAL / FIRE

Metal is totally single-minded and fire can be very demand-
ing, and together this creates an erotic and powerful partnership in the home. You both have a highly developed sense of
ego, and there could be power trips both in and away from
the bedroom. With action and diversity in your distinctive lifestyle, though, this is an exciting and dynamic relationship.

Earth cures are essential here. For good sexual harmony,
spray perfumes or exotic scents over the bedsheets and
pillows. Keep a collection of comedy or blue films for late-
night viewing—humor is essential to lighten up your volatile
energy flow. Keep a bowl of fruit near the bed for erotic late-
night tantalizers. One of the most energizing cures for you
both is to place a piece of pink tourmaline in the southwest
corner of your home to activate awareness of each other's
needs. Bring earth into the home via color (ochres, yellows,
russets) and nature. Choose plants with strong sculptural
qualities, or fossils, shells, and still-life paintings.

METAL / WOOD

In the elemental cycle, metal destroys wood, and these
elements have opposite values—metal requiring ambition
and convention, wood needing freedom and new ideas to
grasp—so this will be an up-and-down relationship. Metal
likes to assert its ideas, and wood prefers to avoid those
who believe they can assert themselves in this way. As with
any polarity, though, there's a strange attraction toward each
other's very different qualities.

For excellent sexual harmony, make sure your bed faces north, and introduce water colors into the bedroom, such as shades of deep blue or inky black, plus a contrast of a fire color to add a splash of passion, perhaps fuchsia or geranium red. These cures can be combined in fabrics, cushions, bed drapes, and covers. This combination will inspire wood's sense of cool detachment and metal's sense of eroticism. Warm up your emotions by placing a piece of carnelian beside your bed and an image of a green dragon above your main doorway for dynamic loving.

⊁ METAL/EARTH

Sensual and receptive earth adores metal's erotic sexuality. This is a good combination of energies, but there are times when you can both be inflexible and self-absorbed, leading to miscommunication. Earth needs security and a loyal and strong partner. In the home, earth can be very possessive about belongings, but metal gives genuine support and is usually the power behind the throne.

The major problem is that metal and earth often spend more time discussing their business or financial affairs than sharing their sexual or romantic needs with each other. To lighten up the heavy energy, bring fire energy into the bedroom in the form of red candles or bright vibrant colors in images or in soft furnishings. Think about steamy nights and tumbling around in colorful cushions rather than sitting in a cool and minimalist room. Place a piece of amber on your windowsill to draw out difficult energies, and a piece of amethyst near your bed for complete surrender.

METAL/WATER

The metal/water relationship is a challenging one, but sexual sparks still fly and the attraction factor is such that each finds the other irresistible. Water is romantic and sensitive, dreamy and elusive; metal is astute enough to recognize these mood changes. Metal always maintains a solid and reliable base for water's more drifting, restless desires.

Use soft colors in the bedroom, such as pistachio, pepper-mint, and almond blossom, fabrics, bedcovers, or drapes in lavender blues, or billowing muslin curtains and flowing fab-rics such as voile and silk around the bed. Introduce strong, fast-growing plants that don't droop (trailing plants can drag water's energy down and depress metal). Introduce the missing earth factor in the form of a bowl of natural stones. Add a piece of azurite in the southwest corner of your home to clear away old memories and any negative energy that may be blocking your mind or feelings.

WATER/WATER

In a water/water relationship, you've both got such change-able natures that you find it difficult to make decisions. There's an intangible quality to this relationship, and you often block out the problems of the real world and drift aim-lessly through life together. Yet you're both highly intuitive about the other's sexual and emotional needs.

Wood cures need to be introduced to help you deal more efficiently with reality and to help you make decisions. Find a piece of driftwood for the southwest corner of your living room, place a carved wooden statue or a four-poster bed in your bedroom, and put a pile of books in the south corner of your home. Introduce images of landscapes and forests or plants in the bedroom. Add some fire cures to boost the sexual passion between you by using red candles, fake-fur rugs, and crimson velvet cushions to bring out the eroticism between you.

WATER/FIRE

The water/fire relationship is a steamy one, and with such opposing energies in action, there are sure to be clashes right from the start. Fire wants to know answers and is always seeking new ideas and responses from his or her partner, but water doesn't like to give much away and won't open up in the passionate way that fire would like. However, fire likes to be in control of the relationship and water likes to be led, so sexually this can be a highly erotic and romantic rapport.

To vitalize such totally different energies, use colors like strong terra cottas or fruit and plant colors like mulberry, sage, ochre, or orange. Introduce wood cures to the bedroom to harmonize and encourage better communication about your sexual needs. Start a bedroom library, or place a pile of books beneath the bed or on a shelf by the window. To inspire each other in daily life, put a small piece of jade or smoky quartz in a velvet bag and place it on a ledge or shelf in the north corner of your home.

WATER/WOOD

The water/wood relationship matures with time, and both of you can relate well to the other's need for space and for novelty. Wood's fear of intimacy feels relaxed and comfortable to the laid-back water personality, and water can drift along with wood's ambivalent attitude to life without making too many demands. There's a powerful connection here, and for excellent sexual harmony, the addition of both earth and metal cures will boost not only your sex life but also your sense of companionship.

It's important that you don't live in a basement or noisy neighborhood. This is not good energy for either wood or water, as both these elements need space and tranquility. If you have no choice but to live in a cramped area or one that is below ground level, place a piece of green tourmaline or lapis lazuli in the core area of your home, as they both emit a powerful protective energy. If you happen to have been born in a metal year, you should avoid adding large metal items to your rooms, as doing so will create an imbalance. However, metal cures will enrich your mutual integrity and goal orientation if introduced in gilt-framed paintings, silver- or gold-threaded fabrics in the bedroom, or a bowl of coins in the south corner of your home. Earth can be incorporated in the form of incense, natural oils, or loofahs and natural sponges in the bathroom.

WATER/EARTH

The water/earth relationship makes for a difficult exchange of energy, as earth is essentially static and water is always changing. The energy between you may become more like a muddy pond than a flowing form of passion if you don't learn to communicate your true feelings. Water needs to flow away and earth needs to feel physically moved. Water can give earth the giddy romance that this element truly longs for, and earth can provide a solid and reliable base for water's more unpredictable lifestyle. It's not an easy relationship, but it is a fascinating one.

To maximize your energy flow, make sure you have music in the home, wind chimes in the southwest corner, and fire imagery (like red balloons rising in the sky, or a picture of a fiery sunrise) in the bedroom. An open fire in your main living area promotes excitement and passion between you. Bring metal cures into the home to keep you both aware of each other's different rhythms. Choose earthy metals such as wrought-iron chandeliers or bronze and pewter goblets, bowls, or sconces to hold scented candles. Place a piece of malachite or white quartz crystal in the west corner of your bedroom for inspired passion.

FIRE/FIRE

The fire/fire relationship is an exuberant partnership. You're both energetic, passionate, and ready for adventure, and this is a romantic, audacious, and provocative relationship. The only downside is that you're both headstrong and impatient, so if one of you gets restless or bored, there is a risk of being led astray or being led into seducing someone new. Fire people need sexy companionship and they need to be adored, but they are not so good at adoring or being deeply emotionally involved with partners. This is a splendid combination if you enjoy fun and games.

Earth cures can be incorporated in the home to give you a chance to come down to earth and be more practical about your financial affairs or your long-term needs. Living constantly for future possibilities means you miss out on the present. Place a bowl of figs, peaches, or apricots in your bedroom, or eat oysters and drink champagne as an aphrodisiac for great sexual rapport. To keep the flames of passion from straying, place a silver-edged mirror in the west area of your home and hang a crystal in your hall or entrance to augment loyalty and commitment.

FIRE/EARTH

The fire/earth relationship makes for an interesting rapport because fire admires earth's ability to get things done, and earth loves fire's enthusiasm and creative ideas. Somehow, cautious earth and rash fire create a dynamic that is mutually supportive. The downside is that you both have very different energy flows, as fire is fast paced and impatient, while earth is slow and sensual. This can be frustrating, but it is also highly original.

For sexual harmony, it's important to incorporate wood cures into the bedroom, whether in the form of a wooden sculpture or a four-poster bed. To ground fire's reckless attitude and vitalize earth's sensuality, place a piece of onyx under the bed. Climbing plants can be placed in the west sector of the home, and add metal in the south corner of your living room in the form of a black-and-white photograph, engraving, or brass rubbing to activate mutual integrity.

FIRE/WOOD

Smooth, sophisticated, and yet romantic, both fire and wood identify with personal space and freedom. Neither gets too hung up about the emotional side of relating, and each thrives on madcap ideas, adventure, and having fun. The idea of using Feng Shui in the home may be too much of a drag for fire, because fire can't be bothered to spend time thinking about it, but wood will spend all night figuring it out!

Metal cures will help you to focus on the aspirations you hope to achieve and give you both the ability to ground your goals. Use black-and-white fabrics in the bedroom, and introduce bronze, stainless steel, or silver objets d'art into your main living area. Place a white quartz crystal or a diamond, if you're lucky enough to have one, on a windowsill in the southwest corner of your home. This will keep the power of your instincts in harmony with the passion of your independent needs.

WOOD/WOOD

Too much wood makes for an unconventional relationship, and while that's okay for some, it can be too unsettling for others. Wood is fine for those who don't like routine living, and who want to spend their time traveling the world or putting the world to rights.

For a creative sex life, bring sensual earth into your home with a glass jar of shells, coral, pebbles, or crystals. Decorate your home in simple colors—whites and creams or duck-egg blues—to give you both a deeper sense of commitment. Gold is a valuable energizer for eternal romantics, so introduce bedcovers or drapes with gold designs or threads. For sheer indulgence, have a huge mirror that reflects daylight in the south corner of your home. To maximize sexual harmony, place a piece of rose quartz crystal on the windowsill near your bed.

WOOD/EARTH

There are very different energy flows in the partners in a wood/earth relationship. Earth is dogmatic and essentially conventional about love relationships, while wood is outgoing, flexible, and unpredictable, preferring to rebel rather than conform. However, the chemistry between you can be erotic because of your very differences. In the home, earth excels in sensual surroundings, while wood prefers a more minimalist atmosphere, so great compromises will have to be made to create harmony.

Don't encourage too much metal in the home, as it's destructive to wood; however, it's highly beneficial to earth, so introduce a little subtle energy with wind chimes. Fire can energize your sexual dynamics, so add candles and mirrors to your living area. Use reds and deep midnight blues or inky colors in fabrics and cushions. Place a piece of amethyst in your bedroom where the sunlight can activate the crystal's quality of trust and enhance your awareness of each other's needs.

EARTH/EARTH

The earth/earth relationship is a highly erotic partnership, both sexually and creatively. Both of you do understand intuitively how to please the other, and you're both driven to create a materialistically sound and secure lifestyle. However, because you're both stubborn and determined to prove a point, there may be the odd sticky moment of sulks and silences. But the earth moves easily for you both, and whether making love or making money, you can get your act together.

Ensure that you incorporate water cures to activate a more flexible and dynamic energy. If you can't cope with a bubbling fish tank, use images of waterfalls, oceans, and even rainstorms. Other water cures can be added using images of fish, or paint the walls in deep inky colors if you dare. Use velvet curtains and dark sumptuous fabrics in your bedroom. Add a little fire to bring sparkle and spontaneity to your love life with mirrors in the living area. In the bedroom, place a piece of azurite to clear away the past and inspire you for the future.

Sometimes nothing can stop a relationship from falling apart. If you have attempted the Feng Shui cures, discovered that trying to change the other person won't work, and found that efforts to change yourself just makes you miserable, call it a day and move on. Then use meditations that will help you to cut away from the past and open the door to a bright new future.

14

CAREER, PROSPERITY, AND BUSINESS

The north sector of your home is concerned with career matters, so you might have already introduced the simple cures mentioned earlier in this book. However, if you want to create opportunities for finding a better job, getting a promotion, or simply developing your reputation and image, you need to do some more work in this area. Below are some Feng Shui tips that are specifically aimed at career advancement or business success.

✗ BEDROOM TIPS

You may be surprised that I suggest that you start by working on the bedroom, but you need to encourage beneficial Ch'i to vitalize your mind and keep you aware of your own level of success and achievement even while you sleep. This will also attract success to you. Don't sleep with your back to the door, and don't sleep under a joist or beam, as this can lead to quarrels with colleagues or difficulties with bosses. You don't need to be blamed for the mistakes that others make. Try to sleep with the headboard facing your most auspicious direction.

The position of your chest of drawers or dressing table is important, too, because this is where you prepare yourself for the day ahead. Facing your most auspicious direction when you get dressed every morning will exert an empowering impact on your work during the day. Just make sure the mirror doesn't face your bed.

In the northern corner of your bedroom, place a bright light or a metal cure, such as a gold- or silver-framed painting, or copper or brass wind chimes. Always check for protruding corners of furniture or hard angles of footboards or walls. To deflect this secret-arrow energy, hang soft fabrics over the edges or the corners, or place a plant in front of the angle to create spirals of beneficial Ch'i. However, never place earth cures in the north corner of your bedroom, as earth destroys water in the destructive cycle of elements.

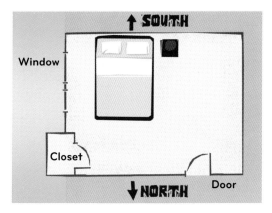

Auspiciously arranged bedroom: the closet here is a projection of the northeast area (education and knowledge).

OUT AND ABOUT

Traditionally, most people who have a profession, career, or business spend a good portion of the day away from home, but these days many people work at home. The following section can be applied to your workspace, at home or elsewhere, because Feng Shui goes with us wherever we go. Each person has his or her own unique energy field, so it's important that when you're negotiating a deal, meeting clients, going for an interview, entertaining important contacts, or simply getting on with your business you're facing your best direction. If you don't know which direction you're facing in a conference room, for example, or when being introduced to a new client in his or her office, take a small compass along and figure out what direction you're facing. Try to sit facing your most auspicious direction to maximize your success; use this direction in all important business meetings.

AROUND YOUR OFFICE OR STUDY

Offices, too, should be arranged in such a way that they have optimum layout; bad layouts, of course, will create bad energy.

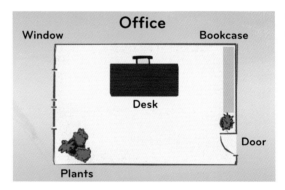

Good office layout.

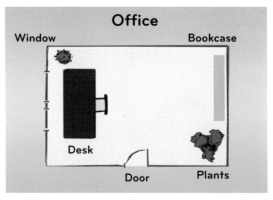

Bad office layout.

Favorable Desk and Work Locations

It's obviously important to be focused, sensible, and calm at work. You probably have to make lots of decisions, or perhaps deal with people who aren't the greatest diplomats in the world. So the direction you face when working in an office is highly important. The other beneficial tip is to always introduce softeners to your office, such as plants to absorb all the secret-arrow energy from angular office furniture, bookshelves, and window blinds.

If you sit in your most auspicious direction and if you can also manage to have a view of the door, this creates excellent energy for clear thoughts, good client contact, and personal success. Never sit with your back to a doorway or window if you can help it, as it can make you feel uneasy.

Kua Directions

1. Take the last two digits of your birth year and add them together. For example, if you were born in 1970, then you'd add 7 and 0, to equal 7. If the result is greater than 9, add the two digits together to get a final result of a single digit.

2. If you're a female, add 5 to the number that you have produced. For example, 5 + 7 = 12.

3. If you're male, subtract your answer from 10. For example, 10 – 7 = 3.

4. If the number you end up with is greater than 9 (as in the female example, above) add the two digits together and reduce them to one. For example: 1 + 2 = 3.

5. If the answer is 5 and you are male, your most auspicious direction is the same as it is for number 2.

6. If the answer is 5 and you are female, your most auspicious direction is the same as for number 8.

Example 1

1. Warren was born on January 17, 1984.

2. The Chinese New Year was February 2 in that year, so he has to move his year of birth back to 1983.

3. He adds the last two digits of his year together: 8 + 3 = 11.

4. He must now reduce this to one number: 1 + 1 = 2.

5. He now takes 2 away from 10: 10 – 2 = 8.

6. Warren's *kua* number is 8.

Example 2

1. Darcy was born on September 28, 1987.

2. She now adds the last two digits of her year together: 8 + 7 = 15.

3. She must now reduce this to one number: 1 + 5 = 6.

4. She must now add 5 to the number: 5 + 6 = 11.

5. She must now reduce this to one number: 1 + 1 = 2.

6. Darcy's *kua* number is 2.

Kua Best Directions

1. Southeast
2. Northeast
3. South
4. North
5. (Male) Northeast
   (Female) Southwest

6. West
7. Northwest
8. Southwest
9. East

You can also create more dynamic success by keeping the desk free of clutter and by adding a metal cure in the north corner of the desk (three coins are highly auspicious).

Computers

Computers are yang activators and are therefore auspicious in your office (but never in the bedroom). Computer screens generate a lot of energy, but too much can overdo the yang energy so that you literally burn yourself out with too much work. Balance heavy computer energy with a yin color scheme such as soft shades of blue in the furnishings, or add plants to soften and calm the highly volatile yang energy.

The Wealth Corner

The southeast corner of your office is concerned with wealth, so, as you would in your home, enhance this corner with a water cure. For example, set up a tank of fish, a small water feature, or a photo or print image of moving water. Goldfish are symbolic of wealth (gold) and happiness (red). Always use an odd number of fish.

15

CAREER CHOICES

YOUR CAREER LOCATION

You can use the Bagua in a different way to bring you good fortune and progress in all your personal vocational needs. Some of us want an easy life and more time to play, while others want a high-powered job or the leadership of a large company. These aspirations can change at different stages of your life, of course; for instance, your focus may be in one direction while you are bringing up children but may change once your children are grown. You may want to alter and modify the kinds of cures that you use as you change and develop. For example, if right now you want an easy job, introduce cures that harmonize the west sector of your home. In six months' time, you might want a freelance job, so you'd introduce some boosters to the north part of your home instead.

The Bagua shows qualities that relate to each of the eight compass points and locations in your home. Look at the words and phrases and decide on those that best describe your situation now; also look at the descriptions that feel right for you at this time.

IF YOU'RE FIRE

Fire people improve their chances of success in their chosen field when wood cures are introduced into the career style location, with a touch of earth to let the energy flow. In the cycle of elements, wood feeds a fire and therefore creates a passion for what you're doing. Earth draws on fire to create a balance. Never overdo cures. If you start filling the career style location with a library's worth of books or green walls and a million plants, you'll simply create an overload.

1. Choose one of the wood colors in this sector of your home, which means forest green, sage, rosemary, olive green, thyme, cool peppermint, or soft pinky hues like the early-morning sky.

2. Choose an earth color, such as twilight blue or pistachio, tones evocative of meadows, light ochres, and the colors of autumn. If you can't see trees or gardens from this location, hang a photo or picture of a landscape beside the window.

3. Introduce a wooden sculpture or a gnarled piece of driftwood into the career style location. If you don't like wood, compromise with a sculptural plant such as a ficus or mother-in-law's tongue (also called a snake plant).

4. Images for the wall can be either bold and direct line drawings or soft hues of watercolors. Books are also a good source of wood energy. Although amassing a library of books isn't ideal because it puts the energy out of balance, add a mural of false books or one shelf of your favorite novels. Don't pile them up on the floor, though, as this creates downward secret-arrow energy that will bring you down to earth with a bang.

5. If the career style location happens to be in the bathroom, then wood and earth cures really do

come into their own, because you can use shells
and natural items such as loofahs and sponges.

6. If your chosen career style location is in the
   kitchen, fill old glass jars with cinnamon sticks or
   coriander seeds. Anything that comes from the
   ground can be lined up on a kitchen shelf.

7. Finally, a single metal cure can be integrated into
   the career style location to ensure success and
   belief in yourself. Add a touch of gold paint or a gilt-
   framed picture. If the career style location is in the
   bedroom, gold jewelry or costume baubles hung
   from your bedpost or laid beside your bed will do
   wonders for promoting positive energy in your
   mind while you sleep.

IF YOU'RE EARTH

To activate your career style location, you need to introduce
fire and metal cures to balance your earth energy. Too much
wood can drain your energy, so if this part of your home
is filled with wooden furniture or plants, try to relocate as
many of them as possible. Incorporate fire cures such as
red candles and subtle but crystal-clear lighting. There is so
much choice of lighting these days that you can easily treat
yourself to something that isn't garish or too bright but that
gives a luminous quality to the location.

1. If your career style location is in the kitchen,
   use stainless-steel cooking equipment,
   and if you can afford to do so, invest in a

stainless-steel work surface. Designs in gold leaf or gold paint or gold-threaded fabrics are excellent metal cures. Some artistic scrap-metal pieces in the corresponding area of your backyard or even the bathroom can be a powerful image of metal that will give you spirit and confidence in your goals.

2. Choose one vibrant color and one softer tone to complement your earthy spirit. Try toning your walls with color washes and tints against dramatically different woodwork. Fiery colors like Indian reds, brilliant whites, crimson, even tangerine will add zest to your career plans. Use one water color only for drive and pure motivation, such as a dark mystical violet or Prussian blue or black.

3. If the bedroom is the focus of the career style location, introduce cushions made from dark damasks or old French-style tapestry. A metal cure here, such as a cast-iron bedstead or gold-framed painting, will induce strength and determination to succeed and will create powerful energy for clarity.

IF YOU'RE METAL

To activate your chosen career style location, you need to harmonize this part of your home with water and earth cures. Earth will instigate realistic values and strength of purpose toward your goals, and water will give you a true sense of achievement and intention to act.

1. Place shells that you've bought or found on a beach, smooth pebbles, or weathered stones in a bowl in the career style location of your home. Flint is especially energizing for metal, but if you can't get hold of flint, buy an unpolished piece of amber and place it on the windowsill. A woodland image on the wall will also bring earth energy into the location.

2. If your career style location falls in the kitchen, you can line up all kinds of natural products on your shelves, such as spices, dried herbs, and jars of rice, couscous, or lentils.

3. A painting of the sea, a photo of waterfalls or surging rivers, or a simple Japanese landscape will vitalize your career style location with water's communicative and proactive qualities. Water colors on the walls will depress someone of your elemental group, so instead place a bowl of blue marbles on the highest surface in the room. You may not be able to see the dark blue hues, but they will be working on your behalf. Add one of earth's warm terra cottas, yellow ochres, or rich umber to your color scheme in this location to help you to understand and relate better to other people as you develop your career potential.

4. To capture the essence of water, if your career style location falls in the bedroom, introduce fabrics, blinds, cushions, or bedcovers that have a hint of blue. Avoid wrought-iron furniture because while it represents your element, it will become a highly charged magnet and confuse your sense

of commitment and integrity. Place a pink shell or rose quartz crystal by your bed to bring you a sense of love for your work rather than the sense that it is just a means to an end.

IF YOU'RE WATER

To boost your career style location, you need to introduce metal and wood cures. Hollow metal wind chimes are highly beneficial to your career style location, as are gold and silver coins, gold-framed photos, black-and-white images, or silver-threaded cushions and jewelry. Place a piece of malachite on a windowsill to enhance the integrity and purpose of metal energy, as this will do wonders for boosting your career opportunities in your chosen field.

1. Wood animates your awareness of what you can and can't achieve. We all have limitations, and wood cures allow us to accept them rather than trying to be too idealistic. Find a wooden carving of a bird because birds symbolize the ability to fly toward your goal with no hindrance. Alternatively, incorporate wooden furniture or sculpture to activate this area. However, avoid overstimulating your career style location with too much wood, as you will end up not really sure about where you are going!

2. Music is a fantastic cure to promote stability and rhythm in your career development. It also reduces your oversensitivity about dealing with

people. Again, you can use wind chimes, but also introduce a musical instrument to this area of your home. Even if you don't play an instrument, buy a recorder, an old flute, a tambourine, or another instrument that you find in a secondhand store, or just play music in your career style location. If it happens to be the bathroom, then sing in the bath.

3. Use wood and metal colors to complement each other, for example, soft greens and a touch of silver, gold, or bright white. Introduce stainless-steel objects if your career style location falls in the kitchen or bathroom, and use plants that are upright rather than floppy. Trailing plants tend to depress energy, and they will make you feel that you're going nowhere fast. Upright sculptural plants are vitalizing and beneficial for career direction.

IF YOU'RE WOOD

To activate and boost the career style location of your home, you need to introduce both water and fire cures. Fire is all about brightening up the location to bring you clarity and focus.

1. If your career style location falls in the kitchen, make sure you have a powerful light source when cooking or entertaining. Hang a string of dried chili peppers on the door or wall.

2. If you don't have an open fireplace in your career style location, then you can always hang paintings

or photos of fire scenes—anything from a mellow bonfire scene to a cosmic explosion of stars.

3. If your career style location is in the bathroom, light candles when you bathe or listen to music when you're washing. Choose "fire tunes" such as "Smoke Gets in Your Eyes," "Ring of Fire," or "London's Burning." If you're working with your bedroom, try to find an old piece of stained glass and lean it in the window to catch the sunlight.

4. Water is highly auspicious in your career style location; it can be incorporated as an aquarium or fish tank, or if the location happens to fall in the bathroom, use an elegant bath or basin, or fish images on the tiles.

5. Find or draw pictures of dragonflies or frogs, and incorporate water colors such as deep blues and inky blacks into your décor or soft furnishings.

6. If your career style location is in the bedroom, hang paintings of waterfalls, fast-moving streams, or waves rolling onto a beach. Use blue carefully in the bedroom, as it can create disturbed sleep patterns. A touch of rich royal blue and deeper violet can be introduced in fabrics and curtains. Lastly, introduce some coral or a piece of amber to the bedroom to give you strength of purpose and induce good decision making in your chosen field.

INTERIORS AND DECORATING

This chapter provides a rundown of how to use color and décor in your home to balance the general energy. It's a useful source of ideas for creating harmony for your own element and for improving your environment. It also tells you how to use colors successfully and when to avoid certain shades.

COLOR ASSOCIATIONS WITH THE BAGUA

Red:	Fire
Orange:	Fire
Yellow:	Earth
Ochre:	Earth
Brown:	Earth
Green:	Wood
Turquoise:	Wood
Blue:	Water
Violet:	Water
Black:	Water
White:	Metal
Gold:	Metal
Silver:	Metal

Red Shades: Fire

Red is exciting; it stimulates rather than moderates, so it must be used with care. In some cases, reds and associated tones such as purple and pink can add spice to your love life or add a dash of drama and intrigue to a dull lifestyle. Handle this color with care, though. Don't use too much, or you could encourage angry and destructive feelings rather than dynamic energy. In nature, red is rare, so always use it

in small quantities, in soft furnishings and fabrics or in glassware or china that is decorated with rich reds and oranges.

Blue Shades and Black Water

The blue spectrum can be responsible for bringing you down
and giving you the blues. Too much can make you depressed,
when what you need is to get in touch with your feelings and
let them flow. However, you do need some of this color to
bring your home into complete harmony. Black, for example,
could be introduced via black-and-white photos or etchings,
engravings, and line drawings. Blue jugs or dark blue china
in the bathroom will instill a sense of flexibility in your home.
Softer shades, such as a touch of charcoal or a hint of gray-
blue, can augment and channel the emotional and feeling
side of your nature, so that you don't lose touch with your
ego or forget who you are.

Green Shades: Wood

Green traditionally moderates our senses and allows us to get
in touch with our roots and inner spirit. Trees and plant life are
obviously valuable sources of green. In fact, natural greens, as
in potted plants and vegetables in the kitchen, are far more auspicious than putting green on the walls. Too much green can encourage daydreaming and idealism, however. Delicate shades
of green can be integrated into the décor. A highly auspicious
place for green is the front door, as this is our access to the outside world and it can welcome beneficial Ch'i into our homes.

Yellow and Earth Shades: Earth

Yellow symbolizes inspiration and beliefs and energizes our
sense of reality. Bright yellows work well in kitchens and

hallways, but yellow is too stimulating a color in the bed-room. Yellow can encompass all the earthy shades, too, including honey, chestnut, and ochre. Spring flowers are often yellow, but instead of thinking only of daffodils, try finding yellow flowers or abstract designs that add a touch of yellow to fabrics and furnishings.

White and Silver Metal

The use of white and silver can enhance your self-esteem and determination to succeed. However, too much white can create cold, critical feelings among family members. If used subtly throughout the home, white can bring purity and integrity to your goals and aspirations. White is easily incorporated into the home, but silver is a little more difficult. The Chinese associate maturity with silver, so encourage success and happiness by using a little silver in the kitchen and bathroom. You can use silver cutlery, perhaps, or paint silver stars on the bathroom ceiling.

MIRRORS

Mirrors reflect the energy in a home, but they also reflect the energy that you create, so make sure you are putting out good or auspicious energy for your mirrors to reflect.

1. Mirrors should always be kept clean and free from dust, and if for any reason your mirrors are cracked or scratched, it's best to throw them out. If you can't get rid of them immediately, cover them with a cloth and store them somewhere where you can't see them.

2. The bigger the mirror, the more energy is reflected, and the more vibrant the household. Make sure mirrors aren't reflecting negative spots, though, such as cluttered bookshelves, a dirty laundry basket, a trash can, a bathroom, electrical cables, or blank walls.

3. Try to use round or oval mirrors rather than square or rectangular ones, as the latter create hard angles and negative energy. If you have no choice, introduce a water cure nearby to help the energy flow more fluidly.

4. Don't sleep directly beneath or in front of a mirror. A mirror by the bed may enhance your sexual dynamics, but this energy is too active and you'll end up having a bad night's sleep.

Using Mirrors as a Remedy

If your home is not a square or a rectangle but some kind of "L" shape, put mirrors on the *insides* of the walls that back onto the missing areas. The mirrors will create the illusion that something is behind them and thus beyond the walls to which they are attached. The reflection literally brings the missing Bagua area to life.

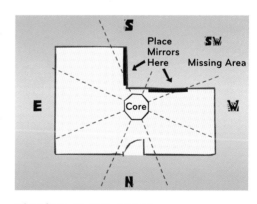

Missing Bagua area:
the east.

In the Far East, mirrors that are used to protect and enhance are in the shape of an octagon, like the Bagua. This shape reflects the spirals of energy, and if placed at the end of a long hallway or on the back door, it enables auspicious energy to stay in the home, while deflecting negative energy or secret arrows back into the environment.

WIND CHIMES

To the Chinese, wind chimes are essential for the generation of good energy and vibrations, and for the Ch'i to flow easily. The music of wind chimes also adds a subtle shift of emphasis to the energy flow in the home. When you buy wind chimes, make sure you really like the tonal quality so that you are in tune with the vibrations.

If you hang wind chimes inside your home, you may find that you don't hear them except in summer when the windows are open and there's a breeze; if this is the case, they won't be of much use to harmonize and circulate the Ch'i. Hang them near the front and back doors or in porches, terraces or verandahs, open carports, or sheltered patios. As long as you like the sound and they don't become a clattering mass of metal clinks every time the wind blows, you will achieve the essence of movement and positive Ch'i. If wind chimes are likely to drive your neighbors crazy, then it's better to find some other way of encouraging good luck into your house.

WATER

Water features are very common in Asian homes and gardens. The water element helps relationships to flow, so it's important not to invite stagnant areas of water into your home. It's fine to have a goldfish bowl or an aquarium, but if the water never gets changed and clouds up with fish waste, what does that say about your life? If you opt for an aquarium, do ensure that you get one with a filter to keep the water crystal clear and flowing.

If you don't like fish, then you can always use a glass bowl of colored water with petals or silver coins in it as your water feature. Alternatively, paintings depicting the sea or a waterfall, or a pond with a fountain or trickling water feature outside your home will create positive and beneficial flow for Ch'i.

LIGHT AND BRIGHT

Bold lighting is yang energy, and it's fine in certain areas of the home, such as the kitchen and working areas, where you need to feel motivated and dynamic. Soft and subdued lights are better in the bedroom, where yin energy is prevalent. Soft candlelight can stir romance and eroticism and generate good relationships.

If you want to enhance yang energy but you hate bright lights, you can always use sparkling objects such as crystals, beads, gems, and shiny metals. Hanging a polished crystal pendulum in your window does wonders for this kind of energy, and the facets of cut glass or droplets from a chandelier are wonderful ways of scattering light across the room into all corners. Ensure that the sun shining on the pendulum isn't likely to start a fire. If you're lucky enough to have stained-glass windows in your house, take advantage of their powerful activating energy. New stained glass is not as auspicious as prewar glass windows because the pigment of the colors isn't as pure. If you do find some modern stained glass in good hues and tones, though, you can place a piece of it in front of a window to energize the Ch'i.

FLOWERS AND PLANTS: SOME DOS AND DON'TS

Most of us have plants in our homes, and this is one of the easiest ways to add the wood element to your environment. However, some plants can be more negative than positive.

- Use flowers that are in season to create vibrant energy.
- Potted plants that come from jungles or rainforests should be used only if you belong to a water element.
- Choose plants that don't take over the home; their invasion can create an imbalance of yin and yang.
- Put a money plant in the southeast and prosper!
- Ivy or anything that trails can turn your well-meaning seduction act or takeover bid into a depressing dream.
- Speckled plants can create arguments between partners.
- Upright plants need lots of space or they can fill the home with arrogance and meanness.

- Dried flowers dry you out, both financially and emotionally.

- Spiky plants invite conflict, but rounded leaves generate positive energy.

ART

Whether you collect watercolors, are addicted to photographs, or prefer abstract painting, keep to your own rules, but do try to modify the amount of wall ornaments you have and where you place them. Adapt your original choices either by adding beneficial elements or by taking away obvious troublemakers from the Bagua areas that are in need of change. For example, if you have an abstract painting (fire) in the north sector of your house, this will create friction in that area. Instead, move the abstract painting to a more auspicious part of the home and replace it with a picture that has a more realistic quality to it.

FORM AND SHAPE

This category encompasses things such as wooden objects, furniture, sculpture, pebbles, natural objects, antiques, and even the television. Inside the house it's easy to place objects such as antiques and furniture, but it is also important to harmonize the outside of your home. This is where natural form can be placed without being too obtrusive. For example, if you found that the missing area of your Bagua was outside your apartment in the communal hallway of the building, then placing a subtle stone or pebble beside your doorway or in the area in question will be enough to restore balance and harmony.

conclusion

Some Chinese people maintain that the original purpose of Feng Shui is to make the spirits of our ancestors happy. Or perhaps it's to please our gods so much that when we get to heaven we settle into the nicest part of it. I guess these are good enough reasons for putting Feng Shui principles into practice, but most of us are more concerned with our daily life than placating the spiritual realm or preparing for our afterlife.

Chinese people are hard workers and they love to make a success of business, so they will spend a lot of money on a complete astrology and Feng Shui consultation for their place of work, after which they call in the decorators to carry out the Feng Shui requirements. We also want to improve our office or work place for business purposes, but most of us also want to make our homes work for us. With Feng Shui, we can hope to eliminate the things that block our progress or suppress important aspects of our lives.

Feng Shui is much like casting spells, smudging with lighted bunches of sage to clear bad vibes or lighting candles according to magic rituals. The idea is to create an auspicious environment for love and luck, and these activities focus our minds and hearts in a way that encourages good Ch'i to enter our lives. We may carry out rituals on occasion, but the effects of Feng Shui are ongoing once we put them in place.

My book doesn't tell you to knock down half your home or to move your front door or your bathroom to a more auspicious area. Instead, I show you how to use mirrors and other ornaments, which we call "Bagua cures," to encourage good Ch'i energies to enter your home and to remain there for good.

I wish you all the best with your Feng Shui efforts, and hope that you get the love, luck, and good health that you desire.

index